The Digital Fundraising Blueprint

How to Raise More Money Online for Your Nonprofit

Jeremy Haselwood

For special orders, quantity sales, course adaptations and corporate sales please make contact through www.JeremyHaselwood.com.

Also available from Jeremy Haselwood are the following self-paced online courses:
- *Digital Fundraising Blueprint*
- *E.D.G.E. Academy*

Visit www.JeremyHaselwood.com for more information.

JEREMY HASELWOOD

Acknowledgements

The process of creating this book is one filled with reflection and gratitude. Reflection of the experiences I've had over the years in fundraising that were full of successes and failures that helped shape the information in this book. Gratitude for the people I've had the honor of working with at fundraising agencies and nonprofit organizations that revealed to me that people are working hard every single day to create more good in this world. I honor the nonprofit employee that is overworked and underpaid because they have the perseverance and heart to work tirelessly towards something they believe in. This book is dedicated to you.

I'd like to acknowledge God for putting the content of this book on my heart and sharing it with those who need it. I would pray oftentimes before writing, that his words would come through, not mine, so that the highest impact can be made from those who read this.

I'm extremely thankful for my family. I want to thank them for their love and support throughout my life. Thank you to my amazing wife Ayonna, and our beautiful kids Amari, Nia, and Jadon. Thanks to my mother, father, stepmother, and stepfather. Thanks to my mother-in-law, father-in-law, and GG. Thanks to my sisters, brothers, and *all* their kids (my fun nieces and nephews). Thanks to my talented Goddaughter. Thanks to all my aunts, uncles, and cousins....until the next reunion!

Thanks to the following marketing and fundraising professionals that took extra time to invest in my marketing career: Chris McKinley, Todd Bemis, Cory Smith, Paul Carpenter, Jason Wood, and Katie Damico

Thanks to all the "students" that have taken my online courses, *Digital Fundraising Blueprint* and/or *E.D.G.E. Academy*.

Thanks to Rebecca Sidener for proofing and editing this book before I released it to the world.

1

Before We Start

Have you ever experienced a day that forever changed your life in a positive way? Not a landmark day that you were expecting – like a marriage or birth of a child. I'm talking about an unexpected day where something occurred that you didn't anticipate that day. One which you had no idea how significant it would be for your life's journey at the time. There's a story to be told about this day, is there not? Well, let me share with you mine, because it's the reason you're reading this book.

When the economy crashed in 2008, things were rough and uncertain for many, including me. I had a college degree and experience with marketing, but jobs were hard to come by. I ended up working a digital advertising sales job because it was related to marketing. Though it wasn't quite how I wanted to use my talent, I didn't have much choice because marketing jobs had all but dried up, and I needed the money. I had a family to support.

I was really interested in working with a marketing agency because I believed it would provide me with the opportunity to use my skills in creativity, marketing, and strategy. So, whenever I saw a role open with an agency in Atlanta, I'd apply for it. I was given a few interviews here and there, but always got the same feedback that went like this: *"We're looking for someone that already has marketing agency experience. You'd have to start in an entry-level position."* Even though I didn't enjoy my current job selling advertising, I honestly felt that taking an entry-level position would be a step back in title and salary, and there were no guarantees as to when or if I'd be promoted.

I saw a job posting one day that was with a marketing agency, specializing in fundraising for nonprofits. The thought alone of using my skills to help organizations do more good in the world was gratifying. I couldn't even imagine having a job where I could put my talents to use and literally change lives. Still, the job seemed unobtainable because it was a marketing agency and, after all, I didn't have agency experience. I applied anyway. Like several jobs I had applied for with agencies, I got an initial phone screener interview. It went well, and they actually wanted me to come in and meet the hiring manager. This hadn't happened before.

Fast forward about a month. I was in grad school, still working at my job, selling digital advertising. As part of the graduation requirements, I had to complete an international residency in Romania for 10 days. The company I worked for knew this, yet they were not going to give me the time off, even though I had enough vacation time. The director of the graduate program even sent my general manager a letter stating that I wouldn't be able to graduate without meeting this requirement. I met with my general manager a few days before I was to leave the country. He told me that, even with the letter from the school, he was not going to let me take off work because of the "needs of the business." He said if I went, then he couldn't guarantee that I'd still have a job when I came back. I had a difficult choice to make.

A few days later, I was on my way to the Atlanta airport. I was feeling stressed and anxious, wondering if I made the right decision. I knew in my heart that I had to make a decision based on my future and not my current circumstances. I believed, if it came down to it, I could find another job. However, finishing grad school would provide me an even better job with more opportunities for personal and

2

professional growth. I knew that in 10 days I might be coming back to a brown cardboard box, with all my belongings in it, waiting for me at my work cube, and turning in my ID badge. Then the phone rang.

On the other end of the phone was the marketing company that specialized in nonprofit fundraising. Long story short, they offered me the job to lead digital strategy for their nonprofit clients! I was so happy, relieved, excited, and looking forward to 10 days in Romania without the cloud of uncertainty, but instead under the sunshine of a promising future. There was a layover in Germany, where I typed my resignation and emailed it to my immediate supervisor and general manager. Rather than dreading it, I was now looking forward to that cardboard box on my desk with all my stuff in it, and being able to turn in my ID. This was the day where something unexpected happened to me that literally changed the trajectory of my life.

My role at this agency launched my career as a digital fundraiser. I already had several years of expertise with digital marketing, but not in the capacity of nonprofit fundraising. Eventually, I would lead digital strategy at another agency that also specialized in nonprofit fundraising. Through my experience, I've met some incredible, passionate people, and seen lives transformed through the money raised online. As of this time, I've been able to help generate over $100 million online for nonprofits.

After meeting with countless nonprofits and fundraising professionals, I noticed that there is a general lack of knowledge of digital fundraising. Sure, there are some agencies that excel at digital, and people in digital roles at some nonprofits that are fantastic. However, an overwhelming majority of my time spent interacting with nonprofit clients was educating them on digital fundraising. I had an epiphany. There needed to be a resource for nonprofit leadership and fundraisers alike to learn the basics of digital fundraising. That's how I came up with *The Digital Fundraising Blueprint*.

The strategies and tactics I've learned over the years of digital fundraising have proven effective in generating revenue. I'd love to help more organizations raise more money to do more good in this world. I've had successes and failures testing different approaches, technologies, and campaigns. The experience shared in this book has taken a lot of bumps and bruises along the way that your organization won't have to take. Sure, you'll have some failures here and there, but you're not starting from zero.

The purpose of this book is to give you the big picture, not all of the details. If I tried to lay out all of the little pieces, as fast as technology moves, those pieces could be obsolete within a period of months. My goal is to give you a broad overview which doesn't change nearly as quickly. It's easier to learn the latest technologies and tactics from trade publications, blogs, news sites, and conferences. However, this book serves to encapsulate a structural overview in one central location based on real-world experience. Let's get started!

Section 1: The Digital Fundraising Ecosystem

2

The Digital Fundraising Ecosystem Overview

Back in middle school, junior high, or high school, you probably learned about ecosystems. You might have learned how frogs, swamps, fish, trees, and the sun were all connected. If you were more science inclined, then I'm sure you took a deeper dive into other ecosystems with organisms I can't even pronounce.

According to Dictionary.com, an ecosystem is a system, or group of interconnected elements, formed by the interaction of a community of organisms with their environment. So what does that have to do with digital fundraising? Everything. The community of organisms are your donors. The environment is a digital environment where people are at home or on the go. The interconnected elements are the different digital marketing channels and how they work to contact, engage, and influence the donor through the donation process. The whole first section of this book explores how simply applying this ecosystem model will provide you with a broad understanding of digital fundraising.

Let's start by first taking a look at the following Digital Fundraising Ecosystem:

THE DIGITAL FUNDRAISING ECOSYSTEM

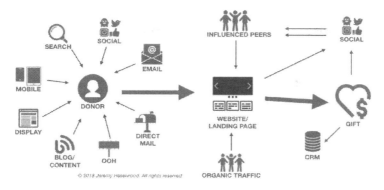

It starts out with the donor in the middle, in his or her regular environment. In the example, we examine eight different **marketing channels**: Email, Social Media, Search Engine Marketing (SEM), Mobile SMS Messaging, Online Display Ads, Blog and/or Content Marketing, Out-of-Home Ads (Billboards), and Direct Mail.

Imagine that these channels are all being utilized with the same marketing message. The donor interacts with each channel differently. In many digital channels, the donor can have an audio and visual experience that is not available via direct mail or out-of-home. Here's an example of how a donor may engage with each channel:

- **Email:** About 10-15% of donors on your email list will open your email
- **Social Media:** 2-10% of donors that follow your Facebook page will see your posts
- **Search Engine Marketing:** Donors and prospective donors searching for terms related to your organization, services, or charity will see your ad
- **Mobile SMS Messaging:** 98% of donors on your mobile list will read your text

- *Online Display Ads:* Donors and prospective donors that are viewing their emails or online content/news sites will see your advertisement
- **Blog and/or Content Marketing:** A donor has bookmarked your blog and visits it frequently to read your stories
- **Out-of-Home:** Donors will see your billboard on the morning or evening commute to and from work
- **Direct Mail:** Donors will get a piece of mail from you, and either open it to read it or throw it away

As you can see, donors and prospective donors interact with each channel differently. Channels like out-of-home and online display ads are great for creating awareness and top-of-mind significance with your brand. Email, direct mail, and SEM are great for a traditional direct-response style of fundraising. Mobile, blogs, and social media content are great for engaging existing donors. Ultimately, all of these channels work to influence the donor in different ways, and also help to amplify the overall message of the campaign. A donor may not have seen your email but may have gotten the direct mail piece at home (and vice versa).

Having a presence in multiple channels helps to ensure that your donor sees the message. Investing only in direct mail, though it has been the cash cow, is essentially betting the house. The same would be true if 100% of your investment were in digital. These days, donors' behavior is not tied to the mailbox. They're on the go, online, and at home. This is why you need a presence in each of their environments. If your organization is not doing this, other organizations will and your donors will dwindle.

Moving through the ecosystem, once the donor gets the messaging through the fundraising channels, they visit the website or fundraising campaign landing page. This is done by either clicking on an online advertisement (SEM, online display, or social media), clicking through a link or call-to-action button in an email, or going directly to your organization's website. Ideally, the donor will end up on the campaign landing page, which has the same look, feel, and tone of the overall fundraising campaign. This helps to provide continuity in the donor experience. This landing page will typically include a form to acquire the donor's credit card information in order to process an online gift.

Once the donor submits the gift and completes the online transaction, a confirmation page typically loads to confirm the gift. This may include verbiage like, "Thank you for donating $50. We appreciate your support." Meanwhile, behind the scenes while the gift is processing, the donor's information is being captured in a secured CRM system that can track or establish your donor's data. More about that later though – let's get back to the confirmation page.

Within the confirmation page, you can invite the donor to advocate for your organization on social media channels. This would allow the donor, while they are in a giving state, to help influence others to also make a donation to your organization. This can be done simply by including words on the confirmation page that say something like, "Please share your support on social media so others can also make a difference." You may also take a more advanced approach that includes coding on your website which allows a pre-populated message to be shared on social media with the click of a button. The second option is easier for the donor, but may require a little more expertise with coding.

After your message is shared out on social media about supporting the nonprofit for which you just made a gift, your friends (influenced peers) and followers will see the message. This message, if executed properly, will contain a link to the donation page, thus driving your friends to the donation or campaign page. Then the cycle continues.

In addition, organic traffic, which is website traffic that happens naturally without direct influence, will also visit your website or landing page. Organic traffic is mostly comprised of people who are using search engines like Google or Bing and searching for keywords or phrases. These people searched words that triggered your organization's website or campaign page to show up in the search engine results.

In summary, here's what happens within the Digital Fundraising Ecosystem:

1. The marketing channels influence the donor to visit the website or campaign landing page
2. The donor visits the website or campaign landing page and makes a donation
3. The donor's data is stored into a CRM system
4. The donor shares on social media with their friends/followers that they made a gift
5. These influenced peers visit the website or campaign landing page as well
6. The influenced peers repeat the cycle of #4 above
7. Organic website traffic visits the landing page or website and makes a donation
8. These new donors repeat the cycle of #4 above

It's really easy when you think about it, right? Of course, this is a high-level view and it's much harder to execute. Also, if it were this easy, I would not be writing a book about it. I'd simply post a blog, dust my hands off, and call it a day. However, now that you have an overview of how all of these channels work together in this ecosystem, we're going to take a deep dive into every one of these pieces. Grab your backpack and compass – it's time to take a journey!

Digital Fundraising Components

As you can see from The Digital Fundraising Ecosystem, there are many moving pieces. The first thing you're likely thinking is "Geez, that looks expensive." In truth, a majority of nonprofits do not have the budgets to run quite as extensive of an ecosystem. Your nonprofit may only be able to do direct mail, email, and social media. And that's fine; do what you can. However, by providing a more comprehensive view, you can get an idea of how it works and how to adapt it to your budgets. Later, I'll go over how to prioritize your digital fundraising investment. For now, let's tee off the following components, then spend time going over each individually:

- Your organization's Website
- Email
- Social Media
- Digital Media
- Blog & Content Marketing
- Direct Mail
- Mobile
- Other Digital Fundraising Channels

3

Your Website, Part 1

Everything starts with your website. It's your online home, and home is where the heart is. Can the world see your organization's heart through your website?

People will go to your website for many reasons, but these are the main ones that I've found to be consistent across most organizations:
1) Learn how to obtain services from your organization
2) Support your cause, i.e., donors wanting to give money to your organization (or see if you're even worth donating money to)
3) Informational purposes – to learn about your cause
4) Volunteer with your organization

With the understanding that these are the primary reasons a person visits your website, the content, messaging, tone, and organization of your site will be the difference between getting help to those who need it or leaving a need unmet.

Website Hierarchy of Content
With a mindset that your website is your home, also consider how you would keep your home if you were expecting guests. The dishes wouldn't be in the sink, bathrooms would be clean, beds made, and carpet vacuumed with those neat little lines. At least that's how it should be, but I can't speak for your home when you have company. I had to clean the house with my siblings every Saturday before we could do anything.

At any rate, you want your website to look clean and people to have a great experience while they are visiting your website. What does that look like? It means the images and content should speak to their heart. You understand why they are visiting your site, and content should be presented in an easy-to-understand way. If a guest visits your house and asks, "Where's the bathroom?" You would probably say, "Down the hall, on your right." Similarly, on your website, they should be able to easily find the content or pages they are looking for rather quickly and easily. On the flip side, if someone asked to use the bathroom, but you didn't tell them where, then they would be left to wander through your house door by door, hoping to stumble onto the correct room. Donors should be able to easily navigate your website as well. Much of this has to do with how content is contextually and hierarchically presented on your website.

Website hierarchy basically boils down to how you organize your site to provide a quick, meaningful experience to your visitors. This means your website should contain menu items that contextually make sense for what people are trying to find. If you know people are coming to your site to learn about the organization, obtain services, or make a gift, then why not include menu items that literally say About Us, Need Our Help? and Donate.

But how do you know why people are going to your site or what type of information they seek? I know you're thinking that question, and there a few ways to do this. If you are using tools like Google Analytics or Google Search Console, then you can find which pages are gaining the most traffic in Google Analytics and examples of terms users are searching to find your website in Google Search Console. You can then organize menus and the layout of your website to coincide with the most frequently searched or visited pages and/or content on your website.

Another way you can gain insight on how to organize and prioritize content on your website is through old-fashioned surveys, of which I'll recommend three. First, and most quickly, you can survey your co-workers and/or family and friends about your nonprofit's website. This will provide a perspective outside of your own as to what they would look for on the site and how easy it is to find it. Another way is to email a survey to your existing donors about their interests or what is important to them. You can take what you learned from a donor survey and inject those findings into your website layout. The last type of survey could be a real-time survey you develop for website visitors that can be done through conversion rate optimization (CRO) tools like Omniconvert or Optimizely. With tools like these, you can create short surveys that pop up on your website to gain information from your website visitors that will help improve the overall user experience.

All in all, the content hierarchy is important on your website because it provides a better user/donor experience by reducing friction in finding the information being sought. In turn, your website is positioned to acquire more donations, volunteers, email subscribers, and more!

Website User Experience (UX)

Related to website hierarchy of content is the user experience, or UX. In fact, I would even say that the hierarchy is a component of the UX because well-laid-out and organized menus and content equal a better experience for the website visitor. I always equate principles of UX to fall in line with The Golden Rule, though modified for context: *Give your website visitors the kind of experience you would like to have if you were going to a nonprofit website.*

UX is very broad though, and I often condense it to identifying roadblocks on your website that delay or eliminate a conversion from taking place. A conversion most often will come in the form of a donation, email sign-up, volunteer sign-up, or a form completion on your website. Here's a roadblock example: If I'm a prospective donor and want to know how much of my dollar goes towards actual services of your organization versus administrative expenses, then I need to be able to find it quickly and easily. If I don't, then I may leave the site before making an online donation. This means your website has a barrier in place which impacts my ability to find information that's important to me as a donor, so now I'm leaving your site. No gift. Nothing!

So, what are the important factors to consider when it comes to UX? I've been involved in numerous UX studies for nonprofits, to where I've landed on five recurring factors. Though this doesn't list everything, if you pay attention to the following items, then you're off to a great start:

1) **Site Speed** – Nothing will kill an online donation faster than a website or donation page that takes forever and a day to load. How many times have you been on a website, seeking to make a purchase, but the website or check-out/payment page loaded really slowly? It happens. But when it happens, you likely leave the site and may or may not go back. The same holds true with your donors. If they have a bad experience on your site or donation page, they may be gone forever.

2) **Content Layout** – This goes back to hierarchy of content, but also how your site looks across mobile and desktop devices. Nowadays most nonprofit websites are optimized for any device, and the content breaks down a little bit differently on mobile versus desktop. The layout should be clean, meaning your images and copy are well organized and not cluttered. In addition, content should be easy to find and website menus very intuitive to an external audience. I say this because I've consulted with nonprofits that organized the content of their

websites around what their internal audience wanted as opposed to the actual *users* of the website, who were external.

3) **Quality of Content** – We'll talk more about content later, but within your website, the most important pieces of content will be the images, videos, and copy that are used. If you remember nothing else I say about quality of content, remember this: *Be Authentic.* Though the use of these two words has become almost clichéd over the last few years, they ring especially true when it comes to nonprofit content. This means you should use real stories, pictures, and videos, and avoid stock images and videos by any means necessary. What this also means is that you, as the nonprofit, must make acquiring and producing content a priority to your organization. Appoint a Chief Content Officer if you have to, seriously. Content is what opens pocketbooks for donors more quickly than any other form of advertising. But it also will kill your reputation faster than high school gossip if you aren't authentic in the content you put out. Powerful stories with phony, posed stock photos are total duds.

4) **Conversion Experience** – The line of demarcation as to whether or not a conversion occurs on your website is usually a form completion. This form may be attached to an email sign-up, volunteer sign-up, Contact Us page, or donation page. The experience your website visitor has with that form will determine whether the conversion is completed or not. It's the difference between making money or losing money, gaining a helpful volunteer or being in dire need of some extra helping hands. One of the biggest barriers to conversion on donation forms is having too many fields. One of the biggest barriers in obtaining an email address is not telling people **why** they should sign up for your emails. If you overcome these two barriers, then you're ahead of the game.

5) **Branding** – Branding equals confidence and trust for website visitors and donors. Some of the nonprofits for which I've completed UX studies had great brand recognition in the

marketplace. Because of this, users of the website pointed out that they trust the site and security of the site because they trust the brand. Even a little thing like not having your nonprofit's logo on your donation page could be a red flag for donors.

Website Branding and Positioning

Your brand is more than just a logo. I really consider your logo as being the face of your brand. Just as you may recognize the face of people you work with, you don't really get to know those people until you spend time with them. This is when you learn their personality, their values, and what makes them tick. All of these different features comprise the person.

Similarly, your organization's brand extends beyond the logo. It's an asset that provides an intrinsic feeling to others, which results from a multi-sensory and emotional experience with your organization. It certainly contains those visibly creative elements like a logo, colors, and tagline. However, your brand contains other elements as well, such as your organization's values, personality, and cause. For example, when people have been helped by organizations like American Red Cross or The Salvation Army, they may have an emotional reaction because those organizations helped them through a time of crisis.

Some organizations have what's called a "sonic brand," which is a trademarked audio sound that accompanies branding assets. Examples of this would be the five chimes that accompany Intel's logo during commercials, the sound a PC makes when Windows boots up and, of course, "You've Got Mail," associated with AOL. More companies in recent years have been adding sonic brands as part of their branding strategy, including AT&T, T-Mobile, and Netflix.

I haven't seen much of this with nonprofits. The closest that comes to mind is the bell ringing around Christmas by The Salvation Army. Though it's not a formalized, trademarked sound that is unique to The Salvation Army, an audio connection exists between the bell chimes and The Salvation Army as shoppers make their runs to grocery stores and malls during the holiday season. In essence, this has become a part of The Salvation Army's brand. If your organization uses a lot of audio or video content in its marketing, a sonic brand may be worth considering, since it adds an additional layer to the brand.

If you're a small or newer nonprofit and haven't formalized your branding guidelines, then you should seriously consider creating what's called a *brand book*. This is essentially a document that provides guidelines on, but is not limited to the following:
- Logo
- Tagline
- Brand colors
- Fonts/typography
- Guidelines on proper use of the logo
- Copy and tone of voice
- Trademark use
- Photography style
- Email signature use
- PowerPoint template design
- Point of contact for branding questions

When it comes to your nonprofit's website, branding is important. The way your brand is portrayed in the real world should be consistent with how it is portrayed in the digital world. This means the base colors of your website should be comprised of those that are part of your brand's color template. Further, the images, tone, and fonts on the website should all coincide with your brand standards. This consistency and continuity of your branding are important because donors assign value to your brand. The value they assign will build or erode trust, and if a donor doesn't trust your organization, then their donations will go elsewhere.

This branding information should sound like common sense, but I'm only mentioning it because I've seen several websites where the colors, tone, and images look nothing like any of the other marketing materials the nonprofit produces. The only consistency was the logo. This isn't to say that different marketing campaigns can't use colors outside of brand colors, but the foundation of the brand should appear consistent across any marketing channel.

In my example of your brand being like a person, imagine if Bob the Accountant always showed up at the water cooler Monday through Friday in a suit and tie. Then imagine one day, perhaps a Tuesday, Bob showed up in a tank top, biker shorts, and flip-flops. And it wasn't Halloween. He's the same Bob the Accountant, but how he's presenting himself isn't consistent with what you're used to. You're left scratching your head. Likewise, you don't want your brand to be "suited up" in the real world but be "casual Fridays" on the website. Be consistent.

Aside from websites, I've also gotten emails from nonprofits that did not sound like the voice and tone of the organization. True story. I once got an email from a humanitarian organization that is known for having a matter-of-fact, serious, and kind of dry tone. That's who they are, and that's who they've been. Well, one day, I got an email from this organization, and upon reading it had to check the calendar to make sure it wasn't April 1; I also double-checked the "From" email address to make sure I had read correctly who sent the email. The tone of the email was as though it were written by an intern with no knowledge at all of the organization's tone. It was upbeat, super casual, and almost offensive. I was turned off, and even wondered if this organization was going through a rebranding, but I would get other emails from this organization that coincided with the tone I'd always known them to have. So, just to reiterate, if your organization's tone is like this:

"During this difficult season, please keep others in mind. Any gift you can make will be a tremendous blessing."

Then don't send an email that says this:

"Hey, it's Friday! You know other peeps out there have it rough this season. We just need a few more donors like you to put some coins together and help others. Be a blessing to others and, boom, blessings will come your way."

I'm only bringing it up because I've seen this happen. On the flip side, if your communication is usually casual and hipster, then sending something overly serious in nature could come off as unauthentic. Protect your brand!

The positioning of your brand on the website is important as well. Brand position is a conceptual place you want to take residence in your donor's mind. On your website taglines, images, stories, and videos, help to shape the positioning. Your positioning is what sets you apart. It's your unique selling proposition (USP) that carefully displays what you do and why you do it. This should be done within the first block of content of your website – using a "hero image" and tagline or other text overlaying the image.

The word "positioning," in itself, is important because it indicates there are multiple positions of nonprofits in an donor's mind. If multiple nonprofits are jockeying for position in your donor's mind and heart, then your organization has a responsibility to shape its position to be the charity of choice for that donor. It doesn't mean that the donor won't give to other organizations as well, but you want to do a fantastic job of telling your story and staying relevant to the donor so you will be top-of-mind over other competing organizations.

Website Email Capture Tips

One of the questions that I most frequently get when meeting with nonprofit fundraising leaders is "How can I increase the size of my email file?" Later in this book, I'll discuss several email list generation tactics; however, at this time, let's take a moment to discuss utilizing your website to capture email addresses.

According to research done by *M+R*, an agency that specializes in nonprofit fundraising and advocacy, around 1% of visitors to your nonprofit's website will convert to an email subscriber. I imagine, through their research, that 1% consisted of a mix of nonprofit organizations that were very good at acquiring emails from the website, and some nonprofits that stunk at it. If 1% is the benchmark though, then the Do's and Don'ts I'm about to share with you should help move that needle a little bit for your organization.

DO:
- Have some real estate on the homepage of your website to acquire email addresses
- Make the email subscribe area easy to find on your homepage
- Give a reason that people should sign up for your email communication, i.e., "Get stories of hope delivered to your Inbox"
- Offer a "freemium," such as a downloadable asset (whitepaper, annual report, tip sheet, infographic, etc.) in exchange for an email address

- Limit the number of fields required on the web form to obtain an email address, such as First Name, Email Address, and that's it (test this)
- Send an email subscription confirmation as soon as possible after a new subscriber signs up
- Use pop-up boxes on the homepage to acquire email addresses, unless it conflicts with the fundraising campaign
- Use exit-intent pop-ups on page in order to acquire email addresses from website visitors that are about to leave your site

DON'T:
- Oversimplify email acquisition by including only one field for an email address and a Subscribe button
- Bury the email sign-up within your website, making it hard to find
- Only use an email icon in the header or footer of your website and expect to grow your email list
- Only offer email sign-up opportunity on the homepage – implement throughout the website where it makes sense for your organization (blog posts, contact us page, etc.)
- Wait too long to confirm an email sign-up – many email tools allow you to automate a confirmation email the moment someone signs up

Getting people to sign up for an email on your website is the lowest-hanging fruit you can possibly access. This fruit isn't even hanging; it's on the ground ripe and ready. Just think, people are coming *to* your website already. You don't need a fancy marketing strategy to get an email address from someone that's visiting your site anyway. Just ask, give them a reason why (the benefit), and watch your list grow.

Donation Page Tips

Your donation page is the last hurdle standing in the way of your donors making a two-way exchange with your nonprofit. The organization gets the money – the donor gets the feeling of doing something good in the world or in benefiting from a tax incentive. Everybody benefits, yet why don't more organizations make this process as easy as possible?

(Stepping onto my soapbox)

Donation page abandonment rates are extremely high. At the time of writing this book, the nonprofit industry average abandonment rate on donation pages was 80% on desktops and 92% on mobile devices *(M+R 2018 Benchmark Study).* For the love of all causes that nonprofits support, please make your donors' experience the #1 priority on the donation page! Stop requiring 30 fields of information that need to be completed, making your donors complete a writing of *War & Peace* before finally submitting their gift. And, for heaven's sake, please eliminate as many distractions on the donation page as possible (i.e., website menus, links to other pages, and social media icons).

(Stepping off my soapbox)

With that said, I'll share with you some donation page Do's and Don'ts. These tips are based on what I've seen as being successful with my own nonprofit clients; however, some nonprofits are unique and buck the trend. I would view these as a baseline, but certainly test for your organization.

DO:
- Reduce friction as much as possible to obtain the gift
- Ideally include only one address field; however, if you include a mailing and billing address, then include a check box that

will copy the address rather than having to type it a second time
- Review your donation page process at least once a year to look for ways to improve
- Include "trust-checkers" like text saying the transaction is secure or use the logo of Verisign or other e-commerce encryption security platform that is used to verify the organization
- Offer a one-time and recurring donation option
- Minimize the number of fields required to make the donation – any other donor information your organization would like to obtain can be gleaned through other tactics
- Utilize the real estate on the gift confirmation page once the gift is complete – this is a great place to have donors share the campaign on social media or take a survey
- Include a statement or graphic about how much of the donor's gift goes to services of your organization
- Affirm your donors through the process by using powerful images or copy at the top of your donation page
- Test gift amounts and gift strings based on your online average gift
- Include "Other" amount in gift string that allows donors to choose the amount they wish to give
- Include impact associated with different gift amounts, if possible – e.g., "$50.32 provides 2 nights of shelter"

DON'T:
- Include a video on your donation page. While it used to be a best practice to include a video on donation pages, I've found that donations actually go down a little bit because more people get caught up in watching the video and then don't have time to donate. A solution you may try is to include a

video on a page by itself with a donate button under the video that points to a donation page.
- Ask for any information beyond what is necessary for the transaction
- Include menu options on the donation page if you can help it – this can be distracting and gives donors more ways to exit your donation page
- Use a donation page that is not optimized for mobile devices

When it comes to your organization's donation page, you want to provide your donors with the same easy experience that you get when you purchase goods or services online. You've likely made an online donation to an organization yourself, so put yourself in the donor's shoes.

Think about Amazon; its process is simple and quick. Challenge your nonprofit to think from the donor's perspective, not the organization's perspective. The organization wants to collect as much donor data as possible so they can have a deeper understanding of the donor. The donor just wants to make a gift and do it quickly. There are other ways to obtain information from donors outside of a donation page, so don't jeopardize the gift in exchange for obtaining information that can obtained through a survey or other measure.

4

Your Website, Part 2

Website Content Tips

The content of your website at a basic level consists of images, videos, and copy. More advanced content may include downloadable PDF files, infographics, or forms. The content used on your nonprofit's website helps to influence website visitors to take an action, whether that's to make a donation, acquire services, or simply learn about your cause.

When it comes to fundraising, nonprofits have a unique product that relies heavily on human emotion and the nonprofit's ability to persuade that emotion to take action (make a donation). Nonprofit companies are filled with passionate people who care about and, in some instances, would die for the cause in which they are employed. However, I've noticed that this passion without business-savvy employees equates to a financially struggling nonprofit. This subsequently limits the impact of the organization, which is counter to why the nonprofit was established in the first place.

I say all of this to nudge you to think about your biggest assets. Of course, the employees of the nonprofit and donors are really important assets. High up on this list of assets should be *stories*. Many nonprofits are sitting on a mountain of stories that are never told. These are stories of transformed lives, improved human impact, goodness in the world, sacrifice, obstacles overcome, and hope. If told, these stories can have a domino effect on the organization. Great stories can reach more donors, which raises more money, which allows more services to be provided, and more impact to take place. This is what every nonprofit wants.

Stories are the content. A key to magnifying impact is prioritizing content creation and distribution of the stories, starting with your website. The following are Do's and Don'ts of website content:

DO:
- Use real photos of real people (or animals) that your organization services
- Get a signed photo release and permission from people to use their story
- Create a role for someone in your organization to oversee the content curation and distribution process – if it's everybody's responsibility, then it's nobody's responsibility
- Approach storytelling from a journalist's lens, with vivid imagery and compelling stories
- Hire a copywriter or freelance copywriter to help write the stories – this is what they're trained to do
- Create a content calendar with themes, story types, and possible subjects (people) of the stories
- Put your best content on the homepage

DON'T:
- Use stock photos
- Post content on your homepage for your internal audience
- Create blog posts without a call to action at the end of it, whether it's to obtain a donation, email sign-up, learn more, or something else
- Keep seasonal or holiday content prevalent on your website when the season or holiday has passed (I'm only saying this because I've seen it happen too many times)

Website Tracking & Analytics

Though many website platforms provide analytics without having to use a third-party platform, my preference, and the industry standard, is to use Google Analytics. This is because of the versatility and depth of the analytics and data, along with the connectedness of other Google services like Google Ads, Google Tag Manager, and Google Search Console. These are all products that Google provides that help with understanding your website behavior and improving search engine optimization (SEO).

Because the Google Analytics platform is so exhaustive in the types of data you can obtain, I'll keep it to a basic level for the sake of this book. As you become more advanced in learning Google Analytics, I'd recommend going through some of the training Google provides directly on their Academy of Ads site: https://academy.exceedlms.com/student/catalog.

If you haven't set up Google Analytics yet, make this a priority for your organization. Start by visiting "Get Started with Analytics" at: https://support.google.com/analytics/answer/1008015?hl=en.

When you sign up, you are provided a piece of web code that needs to be applied to your website. One of the biggest barriers that I've seen for nonprofits when it comes to installing Google Analytics is that nonprofits obtain the code, but don't know how to implement it into the website correctly. Depending on what website platform your organization is using to build and manage content on the site, you may need to have a website developer add this piece of code manually to the site. More and more web platforms, such as Wordpress, are now including a Google Analytics area where you don't have to get into the coding of the website. In this case, you typically only have to provide what's called your Google Analytics property ID, or tracking ID. The code follows a format like this: UA-XXXXX-X (UA stands for Universal Analytics).

The complete code snippet itself looks like this:

```
<!-- Google Analytics -->
<script>
(function(i,s,o,g,r,a,m){i['GoogleAnalyticsObject']=r;i[r]=i[r]||function(){
(i[r].q=i[r].q||[]).push(arguments)},i[r].l=1*new Date();a=s.createElement(o),
m=s.getElementsByTagName(o)[0];a.async=1;a.src=g;m.parentNode.insertBefo
re(a,m)
})(window,document,'script','https://www.google-
analytics.com/analytics.js','ga');

ga('create', 'UA-XXXXX-Y', 'auto');
ga('send', 'pageview');
</script>
<!-- End Google Analytics -->
```

Once your tracking code is correctly set up, Google will start immediately tracking tons of different data points on your website. Google groups the analytics features into the following 6 different categories:
1) Analytics Intelligence
    a. Dashboards with high-level website metrics
    b. Insights that Google automatically introduces to you about trends or opportunities you should be aware of
2) Reporting
    a. Reports from website behavior and metrics can be downloaded
    b. Advertising reports from Google Ads campaigns
    c. Conversion reports, e-commerce funnels, and goal flows
    d. User Flow report that shows the journey of website visitors through your website
3) Data Analysis and Visualization

      a. Filtering and Manipulation: You can customize your data needs through advanced filters and sorting

      b. Segmentation: You can create segments within Google Analytics based on certain website behaviors and monitor those segments

4) Data Collection and Management
      a. Google Tag Management support
      b. User Access – You can control who accesses the data in Google Analytics
      c. Import data from external sources for a more complete view of website behavior

5) Data Activation
      a. Audience demographics, including age, gender, and interest of website users

6) Integrations with the following Google Products
      a. Google Ads
      b. Surveys 360
      c. Optimize 360
      d. Google AdSense
      e. Google Search Console

Some of this may sound like a foreign language to you, so let me break down what I feel is most important to a nonprofit if you're just getting started with Google Analytics. There are five key categories of reports:

- **Real Time:** This is just how it sounds. This report provides data on website visitors that are on your website right now. If you don't get a lot of traffic, then you probably won't view this very often. This tab may come in handy on giving days like Giving Tuesday if you want to see the action on your website as it unfolds.
- **Audience:** This section allows you to view general website metrics, age and gender of visitors, geographic location of

visitors, engagement, what kind of device (mobile vs. desktop) in which users viewed your site, and more.

- **Acquisition:** This section shows how traffic was acquired on your site. Data will include metrics on traffic that come from Google Ads, social media, organic search engine traffic, and more. Here you can compare the quality of traffic that comes from different sources.

- **Behavior:** This section displays how users interact with your site once they are on it. You can identify which pages get the most traffic and metrics associated with those pages. In addition, this section will also show the load speed of your site and suggest improvements.

- **Conversions:** With Google Analytics, you can set up different goals within your site. Goals can vary based on how you define them but may include items like converting visitors to email subscribers, watching 25% of a video, visiting more than 3 pages of your site, acquiring an online gift, and more. You can set up each of these goals within the platform. The Conversions page will show data related to those goals like conversion rate, funnels or paths users took to achieve those goals, and attribution to those goals by marketing channel, based on which marketing touchpoint generated the traffic to your site to complete that goal. The Conversions view is often overlooked by nonprofits because it takes a little more time to set up. However, this can be one of the most insightful pieces of data within Google Analytics that can help you understand your online marketing activity effectiveness.

Each of these categories is filled with tons of information, but not all of it is relevant to your fundraising activities. At a foundational level, there are some metrics and terms that you need to understand when it comes to Google Analytics. Let's take a look at the following screenshot of the Audience Overview screen and review the terms.

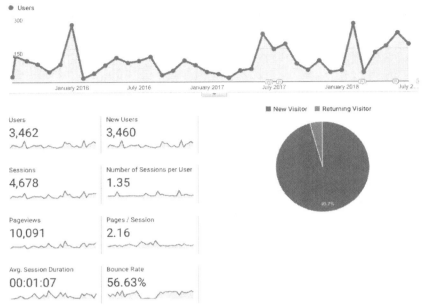

Users: The total number of visitors that visited your website

New Users: The total number of unique visitors that visited your website

Sessions: The number of times your website was visited by your users

Number of Sessions per User: The average amount of times each user visited your website

Pageviews: The total number of pages on your website that all of your users visited

Pages/Session: The average number of pages on your website that were visited during each session

Avg. Session Duration: The average amount of time that users spent on your website during each session

Bounce Rate: The percentage of users that visited your site, then left your site ("bounced") after only seeing one page

New Visitors: The percentage of users that have never been to your website before

Returning Visitors: The percentage of users that have previously been to your website

Now that we've gotten the vocabulary out of the way, let's look at the numbers from this example and try to make sense of it. During the timeframe in which this data was collected, 3,462 people visited your website – 3,460 of which had never been to the site before. These 3,462 people accessed, or visited, your website a total of 4,679 times (1.35 times per person). While these 3,462 people visited your website, they also visited a total of 10,091 pages on your website, or 2.16 pages per person. They spent an average of one minute and six seconds on your site. Finally, about 56% of the times your site was visited, the person left without visiting more than one page on your website. It's certainly a case of following the math.

Taking the basic understanding of these terms, within Google Analytics you can see how these metrics apply to different devices (mobile vs. desktop), geographic regions, and specific pages on your website. Amongst other things, all of this information helps you understand how people interact with your site and where people go once they are on your site. In turn, this can provide insight into the types of content that resonate, and where geographically you may want to focus fundraising campaigns.

In a nutshell, Google Analytics can answer **who** is visiting your site, **how** they are getting there, **what** they are visiting, **where** they are leaving, and **how many** are converting. You have the ability to drill deep into any of these metrics, but at a high level, this allows you to keep a finger on the pulse of what's happening on your website. You might even be able to pair this with some of your direct mail data to improve the overall quality of your fundraising program.

Website Search Engine Optimization (SEO)

Search engine optimization involves the art and science of ensuring your website is optimized to be visible by search engines like Google, Bing, and Yahoo. It's not enough just to be visible by search engines though, the goal is to be the first listing in the organic section on the first page of search engine results.

Let's back up a moment though and talk about the difference between paid and organic search engine results. I will reference Google more in this book when it comes to search engines because approximately 75% of all searches online (in the USA) occur on Google. In the following example, I searched the phrase "donate to nonprofits" on Google. What you see is the results of that search. The top three listings are paid advertisements. You'll notice in small print the word "Ad" appears with an oval circle around it to the left of the ad. Those are ad placements through Google Ads. We'll talk more about that later. The listings that appear below the paid section are the organic search results. These are influenced by search engine optimization of your website.

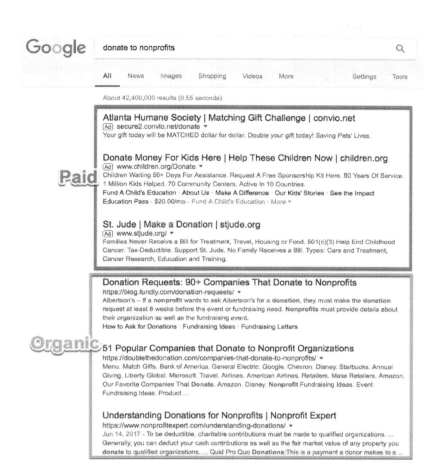

Though outsiders don't know the exact algorithm used by Google that determines what order websites will appear in search results, it's important to understand the goal of Google. Remember, Google is a business that needs people to use its search engine. People will only use a search engine if they can find what they want quickly and easily. If Google doesn't do this, then they will lose users. Therefore, they want to provide search listings that are absolutely the most relevant to what they believe you are trying to find. To do this, they look at two components of SEO – on-site and off-site.

On-Site SEO is a factor that you can modify within the content management system (CMS) of your website (think WordPress). Depending on the CMS your organization uses, you may need a website developer to implement the SEO components. These components are often called the metadata of your website, and include the following:

- **URL Name** – The words contained within the URL of your website. Naturally, your brand name should appear in your website. If your brand name is really long, then initials will work, as long as that's how the public knows you and would search for you online in that manner.

- **Page Title & Description** – Each page of your website has a title and description. This is important because what you put in those fields will show up on search engines. The following example was cut/pasted from search results. The page title is "The Digital Fundraising Blueprint Online Course | 4.5 CFRE Points." The page description is "Gain 4.5 CFRE points and learn all about digital fundraising for your nonprofit, charity, and NGO. Includes email, social media, website content, SEM, and more!" Notice that the words I used in the description included keywords in which I wanted to be found in search results.

  The Digital Fundraising Blueprint Online Course | 4.5 CFRE Points
  digitalfundraisingblueprint.com/ ▾
  Gain 4.5 CFRE points and learn all about digital fundraising for your nonprofit, charity, and NGO.
  Includes email, social media, website content, SEM, and more!

- **Headings and Subheadings** – Website headings and subheadings have a similar functionality as they would a newspaper. For example, your main headline of a newspaper would be bigger and bolder than any other headline on the page. Subheadings in a newspaper would still be large and bolded. This helps a newspaper reader scan the bolded headlines to get an idea of what the article is about and determines whether or not the reader will actually read the article. For websites, Google looks at your headings (called H1) and sub-headings (called H2, H3, H4, etc.) to determine keywords and content relevancy to what users are trying to find. Use of headings, and relevant ones at that, will improve your SEO.

- **Alt and Image Tags** – Parts of SEO that a user typically won't see are the alt and image tags. Generally speaking, these are descriptions that become visible when a user hovers his or her mouse over an image or link on your website. The image tags also appear when images don't load properly to provide context as to what the images contain. These tags are one of the most overlooked components when it comes to improving SEO, often because many platforms don't offer an easy way to include these tags and may require a person with coding experience to help.

Tip: To gain insight on how your page looks in Google search results, set up Google Search Console for your website (https://www.google.com/webmasters/tools/). This will show you keywords, average search results position, click-through rate of your listing, and more!

Off-Site SEO is a factor that impacts your website search results rank, which you cannot control within your website CMS. These are external signals (i.e., data) that search engines find about your website to determine the relevance of your website, based on the keywords or phrases being searched. I typically bucket these into the following four categories:

- **Local Directory Listings** – Search engines will scan the web, including online business directories like Yelp, YP, Google business listings, and more. It's important to not just register with online business directories, but also complete as much of the business listing as possible. Each site has some pretty standard items like a business description, services offered, hours of operation, phone number, address, website URL, and ability to upload a picture. Complete all of this. Just like you spend time optimizing your website for search, you want to optimize your local listings as well. This lets search engines know that: 1) Your organization is an active business; and 2) Your business may be an authority online based on the words that were searched.

- **Authoritative Sites** – Backlinks are essentially links to your website that appear on other websites across the internet. Generally, the more quality backlinks you have on the internet, the higher quality your website is considered to be by search engines. The keyword here though is *quality*. For example, if your nonprofit has a link that appears on gambling, cryptocurrency, or porn sites, then that would likely hurt your website rankings. Quality backlinks would come from sites that have authority such as news and blogging sites. If you were to do a press release or have a story done about your organization that appears on the local or national news, links from that article to your website would have a high level of authority. This helps to build overall authority for your website and improves your rankings on search engines.

- **Bookmarking** – When it comes to your online web browser behavior, it's safe to say "Google knows all." Not just Google though, most popular web browsers know a lot about you. I know, it's scary for you as a consumer, but fabulous for you as a marketer and fundraiser. One way this works to your advantage if you're a nonprofit or other business is that it also knows when people bookmark your website. When people bookmark your website, that action essentially tells web browsers that your site is legit. Naturally, the more people that bookmark your site, the better it helps your SEO as a result. Do you have a bookmark feature in the header of your website?

- **Social Media Accounts** – Most social media content is not searchable from web browsers. This is because the content exists behind a "wall" where you actually have to log into the site to have access to the content. However, search engines can usually see if your nonprofit has a presence in social media. My advice would be to at least grab your social media real estate on as many social media platforms as you can, even if you're not active in all of them. Complete as much of your profile as possible, including images and website URL. This helps to not only establish your branding on each site, but also lets search engines know that you have a pulse in the social media world. You know what I'm going to say next, don't you? Yes, this also helps with your SEO.

Website Privacy Policy, Terms & Conditions, and GDPR
I'll tread lightly in this section because I am not an attorney, nor is any of this to be construed as legal advice. If you have any questions about this section, please consult an attorney for clarification. And with that out of the way, let's talk about website privacy policy, terms & conditions, and GDPR.

- **Website Privacy Policy** – A website privacy policy is not a "nice to have" – it's a "must have." Chances are your nonprofit already has one of these on your site, so this may not be an issue. If you don't have a privacy policy, please research and institute one as soon as possible (perhaps today). If you don't have a privacy policy, then you may be breaking privacy laws and could be subject to lawsuits. In addition, a privacy policy is also one of those "trust-checkers" that let your donors know that you are in compliance with privacy laws and they can trust you. Your privacy policy should disclose what and how you collect, store, and share personal information. This policy should be easily findable, and typically appears in the footer of your website.

- **Website Terms & Conditions (or Terms of Service)** – Terms and Conditions include information that visitors need to know about using your website. This is where you would include arbitration clauses, liability disclaimers, copyright and trademark notices, the handling of abuse of the site, and so on.
- **General Data Protection Regulation (GDPR)** – Though GDPR is a European Union regulation, you may want to follow suit with its requirements because I can see the United States adopting parts, if not all, of the regulation one day. Currently, you only need to be concerned with this if you are a nonprofit that markets in the EU. If you're only marketing in the USA or foreign countries outside of the EU, then definitely be aware of any other privacy policies in which you need to comply. Not only does GDPR spell out what you need to let consumers know about your collection and management of personal data, it also lists steps your organization must take internally to be GDPR compliant. You can read more about it here: https://ec.europa.eu/info/law/law-topic/data-protection_en

5

Email, Part 1

For nonprofits, most started dipping their digital toes in the fundraising water years ago by getting a website. As they started to further submerge themselves into the pool, email was next to go under. When it comes to fundraising, direct mail has always been the swiftest swimmer in the pool. To illustrate, let's just say that direct mail was the master of the breaststroke and king and queen of the pool. Nonprofits wanted email to be like direct mail and also master the breaststroke; however, email was different. Email had its own style – let's say it was the butterfly stroke. And though not as fast as the breaststroke, it was pretty fast with the butterfly stroke and got faster and stronger every year. And when direct mail and email swam together in the pool, it caused more people to pay attention. And the moral of this story is email is not direct mail, but there are some similarities. When they both work together, it's better than them working alone.

When email fundraising was introduced, many nonprofits thought it had to be an exact replication of direct mail, only in digital form. You would see what essentially appeared to be a photocopied version of a direct mail piece delivered to an email Inbox. Pretty? No. Effective? Not so much. I've never seen anyone interact with an email like they do a direct mail piece and vice versa. Donors experience these forms of marketing in different ways, and each marketing channel should play to its strengths.

With direct mail, you can add premiums like address labels or other tangible items. Donors can touch, feel, smell, and turn the page(s) of a direct mail piece. You can't do any of that with an email. However, with email, you can provide slideshows, videos, and motion design elements. An email can come to you on your phone or computer without leaving your seat. It takes a walk or drive to get a direct mail piece from the mailbox. Bottom line, they're different, but they can both tell the stories about your organization in a different way that will engage donors.

Email design and strategies have evolved over the years as more organizations are hiring digital talent or outsourcing digital fundraising to agencies or consultants. Though the nonprofit sector trails behind the commercial sector when it comes to technology and digital marketing, great strides have been made. I believe that top digital leaders at nonprofits can learn a lot from the commercial world and more advanced digital marketing ecosystems, but also must honor and preserve the legacy of the donors of the organizations. It's a fine balance, but necessary to evolve and remain relevant.

Back in the day, the value of an email was that you could reach a donor or email subscriber directly in his or her Inbox. This is valuable because email is a very successful fundraising channel; however, if the email is never opened, then that was your only shot at reaching the donor. Now, an email address can be used to not only connect with donors in the Inbox, but also target donors with social media ads, online display ads, and other pay-per-click ads. This is because, when setting up online ads with providers like Google Ads or Facebook Ads, you can upload your email file into these platforms as a targeted audience. Users of those platforms can be targeted with ads **if** the same email address is used as their login address. In other words, if a donor provided their email address as donorX@gmail.com and that's also the same email they use to login with Facebook, then they will see your ads on Facebook. So, if donors don't see or open your email, you still have a way to reach them with your message in other digital channels. As you can see, the value of an email, this one data point, is far more than what it ever used to be to your nonprofit. This is why acquiring more quality email addresses should be a priority for your organization.

Let me draw attention to the word *quality* for a moment. In the heyday of email acquisition for nonprofits, e-appends (or email appends) were very popular. This is the practice of taking your direct mail donors, partnering with a data company to match your donors with known, existing email addresses for your donors, then providing you with a list of those email addresses. I've got to tell you, those were exciting times for email list growth. I saw email list sizes literally go from a few thousand to a couple hundred thousand – in some cases, just through doing these e-appends. It was amazing because, just like that, a digital fundraising program increased significantly in value.

But there was a problem. When you're building bridges as you cross them, you don't have a precedent to learn from. It's like that in many areas of digital fundraising. In this case, it would be learned that an overwhelming amount of the email addresses acquired from donors were not of high quality. What that means is that some email addresses were old, no longer active, or inactive, meaning that the email address is good, but the person never checks the particular email account.

Initially, it didn't matter much. The industry consensus, including mine, was that "It's more quantity that's important rather than quality." This was because we knew these were email addresses for donors, so the relevancy was there. These weren't strangers to the organization or random emails that were acquired. Besides, if the donors didn't open the emails, there was still perceived brand value to it because they at least saw the brand name of the nonprofit in their Inbox. Not ideal, but still not perceived as a bad situation.

This all changed in 2016. It's a year that will go down in infamy for me because the clients I was working with were directly impacted. When the autumn season came around, tweaks to email deliverability had been made by email service providers (ESPs) like Gmail. This meant the algorithms of these ESPs were modified to refine which emails went to the Inbox and which emails went to the SPAM or Bulk Items folders. Though ESPs had done this on an ongoing basis for years in order to weed out SPAM from your Inbox, this time the changes inadvertently impacted many nonprofits.

In a flash, the days were gone of quantity over quality when it came to the emails on a nonprofit's file. The email files of some of my clients were comprised heavily of email addresses that were chronic non-openers; therefore, a majority of emails, even the quality ones,were now going to SPAM or Bulk Items folders, and never to be seen by the donor. Just like that, the air was sucked out of the value of an email fundraising program. I immediately changed my ideology to quality over quantity and had to retrain my clients on this mindset as well. So how can you keep the quality of your email file intact so this doesn't happen to your organization? I'll talk more about this when we get to email list hygiene. For now, let's get into how and why you should focus on email acquisition for your organization.

Email Acquisition Tips
According to the M+R Benchmark Report, approximately 1% of visitors to nonprofit websites will sign up for email updates. Email acquisition is really a lifeblood to your digital fundraising because: 1) The value of an email address is higher than it's ever been because you can use it to target donors in other digital channels; and 2) The need to backfill inactive email addresses on your file or unsubscribes will preserve email revenue growth. Without email acquisition, your

email file will shrink as will the digital revenue of your campaigns. Let's not allow that to happen.

Remember, it's now about quality over quantity. Don't take the Groupon approach where any email address is a good email address. You want your email file to be filled with subscribers that actually want to hear from you. Here are some ways to acquire new email addresses:

- **Modals, lightboxes, and more:** One of the easiest ways to acquire an email address is through modals, sometimes called "lightboxes," when people visit your site. These are basically pop-ups that appear on your website where you can include an image, text, and form fields along with a "Subscribe" call-to-action button. I recommend implementing a lightbox on your website for *donations* while you're running fundraising campaigns, then revising lightboxes for *email acquisition* outside of fundraising campaigns. One of the concerns I've heard from many clients is that they don't add lightboxes to their site because they think they will annoy donors. True, you'll have anecdotally 1 out of 100 visitors that may be annoyed, but most people are used to these types of lightboxes on websites because it's a common practice. For more information about this, visit https://moz.com/blog/popups-seo-whiteboard-friday .
- **More than an icon:** On many nonprofit websites, it's not easy to find out how to subscribe to receive email communication. If someone has to search through your site to find out how to sign up for your email lists, then you've lost them. One of the tactics I've seen many nonprofits use is including an email icon in the header or footer of a website. While this tactic isn't bad if it's paired with more noticeable email sign-up tactics, using only an icon will not be effective in acquiring many email addresses. There should be a highly visible area on the homepage of the website specifically for acquiring

email sign-ups. In addition, I recommend including email sign-up areas throughout your website, not just on your homepage. Put it on your Blog, Contact, Services, and the rest of your website; however, don't include it on your donation form. For donation forms, simply put a check box that gives permission for you to email them in the future. By making your email sign-up form more visible on your website, you'll start to acquire more email addresses.

- **Give a Reason:** Another fallacy I regularly observe is that when organizations do have a very clear email sign-up form on their homepage, it's too generic. It has a box to enter your name and email address, then says something like, "Subscribe" or "Get Email Updates." While this is far better than just having an email icon in the header or footer, an opportunity has been missed. You want to tell your potential subscribers *why* they should sign up. In other words, what do they get out of it? Always provide the benefit a person will receive by signing up for your emails. This may include something such as, "Get stories of inspiration delivered to your Inbox. Sign up to receive emails from us." I've even seen organizations tell how frequently they send emails and how their emails are used. This would look something like, "We won't send you more than 3 emails a month, and we never share your email with third parties." These tell subscribers what they will receive, the frequency, and how their data is safe. This is a good approach because it builds confidence and sets expectations.

- **Freemiums:** A popular method to acquire email addresses comes from the commercial world. For years, companies have been successful in using freemiums in exchange for an email address. A freemium is a "free premium" piece of content. These are usually things like whitepapers, e-books, infographics, tip sheets, or coupons. In the nonprofit space, what would be something of value to your potential donors that you could exchange for their email address? Maybe it's an annual report, access to an exclusive video, e-book, or downloadable inspirational quotes. Think about what content would be unique to your organization.

- **Surveys/Quizzes:** By using online tools like SurveyMonkey.com or Qzzr.com, you can create online surveys or quizzes. This not only allows you to learn and engage more with your prospective donors, it also is a means by which you can obtain an email address. You can implement these on your website through the use of a lightbox when people visit your website. With surveys, ask important questions that may help you learn more about what's important to your donors. With quizzes, make them fun, engaging, and tied into the purpose of your organization. If possible, obtain an email address after the final quiz question and before the person sees his or her results. If you ask for the email address after the results, you may not have as much success.

- **Donations:** Just because someone makes a donation to your organization, it does not mean that they give you permission to email them. Make sure that your donation forms include a mandatory field for an email address. Then, if possible on your form, include a check box that says something like, "I'd like to receive email updates in the future." Due to evolving data permission regulations, I'd recommend you leave this box unchecked and allow the donor to check it.

- **Events:** Events can be tricky when it comes to obtaining email addresses. It's not so much gathering email addresses as it is making sure these email addresses make it to your email file after the event. Event registration, whether online or in person, is the ideal time to acquire new email addresses. When obtaining email addresses in person, some organizations use paper forms, while others include some form of technology (tablet or computer). Either way, the person registering for the event needs to either accept or reject being put on your email list. If it's a paper form, include a checkbox that asks if the person would like to receive emails. It's also important that the person administering the registration at an event calls attention to the email box. This can be something simple they could say like, "Please check that box so we can communicate with you in the future through email." That's it.

- **Lead Generation Ads:** Facebook provides what are called Lead Ads. Just as it sounds, these ads are exclusively designed to acquire emails for your organization. The ads include a simple form, text, and image. Once a lead is obtained, a "Success" screen appears, which allows you to include a URL that you can share with your new subscribers. This may be a good place to insert a link for more information about your organization, or even a donation page. Of course, this method of email acquisition involves spending money on advertising. To analyze the cost, you would not just look at how much it costs to acquire a new email address. You would also want to track these email addresses to identify how many actually become donors. Only then will you really get a handle on what the cost of *donor* acquisition is via this tactic as opposed to just the cost of acquiring an email. Then, you can compare this cost to what your direct mail donor acquisition cost would be and make decisions based on how you will divide acquisition budgets in the future.

- **Online Petitions:** The use of online petitions can be effective at generating emails quickly; however, sometimes the quality of the emails may not be ideal. This is because people can rally behind a cause but may not necessarily want to get emails from your organization. Online petitions can be quite dynamic, including powerful images, videos, and testimonials. They can also be amplified through digital advertising and sharing on social media. This is something you may want to test with your organization. For the sake of data integrity, I would send the cohort of emails acquired through online petitions separately from the regular email file for at least 6 months to better understand the quality of emails. If email metrics of that cohort appear to be in line with the rest of your email file, then you could add them into the file.

The Anatomy of a Fundraising Email

When it comes to email, your organization's messaging and design should be modified based on the purpose of the email. In fundraising emails, the goal is get **money**. This means that the communication will be more urgent, and there will be direct asks for donations. It's difficult for me to capture in this book what the perfect fundraising email should look like because design, technology, and donor response evolve so quickly. There are some differences between fundraising direct mail pieces and emails though. In direct mail, letters can be long and contain multiple pages. In email, copy should stay relatively short and sweet due to how donors and consumers interact with email versus direct mail.

In addition, I've tested different fundraising email designs and was interested to find that sometimes a designed email with images, colors, and graphics won't raise as much money as a good old-fashioned email that contains little to no graphics and just text. The reverse is also the case. I believe context is the key when it comes to design. The rule of thumb I go by is to have a well-designed email if it falls within a campaign theme. For extra urgent, time-bound appeals, test out a minimalist email with just text. I believe this works because a minimally designed email can appear more authentic to the donor, as if it were sent personally from somebody within the organization.

At a foundational level, I believe somewhat of a formula exists when it comes to the design of a fundraising email. I've laid out the formula in the wireframe below. My only disclaimer would be that this can be a starting point for you if you're starting with nothing. If you already have a formula that works for your organization, then great! You may want to test against what's laid out in this wireframe and see which wins.

Fundraising Email Wireframe

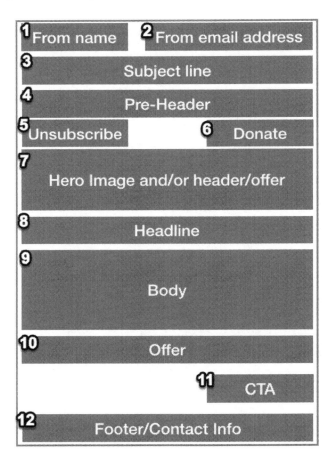

1) **From Name:** This is the name that will appear in the Inboxes of people that receive your emails. Some organizations use just

company name; some organizations use the name of the Executive Director or other leader of the organization. Test these to see which one leads to higher open rates. Also, if you do land on one name that you consistently use in this field, you could also try testing another From Name during urgent appeals. This name should be either the President, CEO, or other leader of the organization. I've tested this tactic before and the alternative name raised more money. This may not work for you, but it's definitely worth split-testing.

2) **From Email Address:** This is the email address that recipients see in their emails. For fundraising emails, you may not want to use a generic email address like info@yournonprofit.org or noreply@yournonprofit.org, as it may come off as inauthentic or as if the organization were unapproachable. I've seen organizations set up an email address with the company's name or a leader of the company's name in the email address. Be careful though not to use the real email address of one of your organization's leaders unless they are open to getting a barrage of emails directly from donors. For example, if your leader's email is janedoe@yournonprofit.org, then maybe the From Email Address could be jane@yournonprofit.org. Just make sure that email is really set up so somebody within the organization can check it regularly in case a donor has a question or comment.

3) **Subject Line:** A good subject line is a critical factor in getting the subscriber to open your email. So many questions abound when coming up with the perfect subject line. Long or short? Question or call to action? Emoticon or no emoticon? The answer to all of these questions is YES. Interestingly, I've seen all of these win in tests within the same organizations. Long subject line beat short subject line, then vice versa. Emoticon in the subject line beat no emoticon in the subject line, and vice versa. You have to test to see what works best for your organization. Then, when you have it figured out, test again. The only rules I really do follow are

don't use "FW:" or "Re:" in your subject lines because those are SPAM triggers. Also, if your email includes a slideshow or video, I'd include those words at the beginning of the subject line like, "Slideshow:" or "Video:." I've seen this tactic consistently outperform subject lines that contained a slideshow or video, but didn't contain those words in the subject line. I also try to keep subject lines to less than 50 characters for better viewing on smartphones, but this is not always possible. You can read all the best-practice blog posts and articles about how to write the best subject lines, but it all comes down to what works for *your* organization. Start with these tips; heck, start with the "best-practice" blog posts, but make sure you find what works best for your email subscribers.

4) **Pre-Header:** The email pre-header is the short summary of text that follows the subject line. While it's visible, it does not usually appear in the email once it's opened; it does appear in the Inbox when subscribers are scrolling through their emails. This pre-header text is important because it provides further context with the subject line as to what the email is about. Use this space wisely, and don't leave it blank when you're building emails. Say everything you need to say in about 100 characters for better visibility on smartphones. Use this space to tease out what the email contains. Your pre-header impacts open rates, so make it such that it peaks the subscriber's curiosity. Also, don't repeat the subject line because that devalues the purpose of having a pre-header in the first place. In the following example of an Inbox view on a smartphone, the pre-header appears with a box around it:

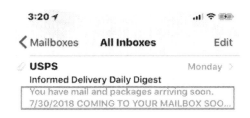

5) **Unsubscribe:** Including an Unsubscribe link at the top of the email is a relatively new approach I've started taking. The reason for this stems from my former mentality of quantity over quality. Though an unsubscribe option is mandatory to be compliant with CAN-SPAM laws (more on this soon), I used to bury the Unsubscribe link at the bottom of the email because I didn't want to lose any subscribers. As I changed my tune to quality email addresses over quantity, I also changed my approach to moving Unsubscribe links to the top and footer of the email. I do this because: 1) I don't want people to flag my email as SPAM because they can't easily find how to unsubscribe; and 2) If people don't want to receive emails anymore, then I'm at peace with that. This protects the health of the overall email file because I don't have a lot of non-opening email subscribers. Lower SPAM rates and higher open rates will improve your organization's reputation with Gmail, Yahoo, and other email service providers.

6) **Donate Button:** This is a fundraising email, so including a donate button in the upper-left corner of your email is completely OK and expected by donors. Honestly, I'm a proponent of including a donate button in that same area on every single email, be it affirmation, fundraising, or otherwise. I've participated in many healthy debates with nonprofit employees and marketing agency folks about whether you should include a donate button on affirmation emails. My take is simple. It's an email from a nonprofit. Nonprofits are only in business if they receive donations. People who receive emails from nonprofits know that nonprofits need money to survive. Including a donate button on an affirmation email is not offensive. I've run tests on affirmation emails with and without donation buttons. There was no increase in unsubscribes and no complaints. I view it as a missed opportunity in incremental revenue if you leave donate buttons off of emails. Maybe that donor didn't have money

when your fundraising appeal was sent, but now they do and make that gift on an affirmation email. Reduce friction and allow that person to easily respond to your affirmation email by making a gift.

7) **Hero Image and/or Header/Offer:** Similar to the homepage on your website, the use of a hero image within email can help engage the email subscriber and entice them to read the email once it's opened. An image helps the story within the email come to life. It puts a name and a face with the need. Challenge your organization on the use of images. If you're just throwing an image at the top of your email for the sake of having an image, then it may not result in a lift in revenue. Your image should be emotional and relevant to what the email is about. A great hero image would include eye contact from the subject(s) in the photo. You might even test the inclusion of a text overlay on the image that presents the offer. For example, text that says "$52 = 2 Nights of Shelter" overlaying the image of a homeless man or family shows the human need and the ask (the offer). The rest of the email tells the story of the subject contained within the image.

8) **Headline:** Also, similar to the homepage of your website, the inclusion of a headline provides context as to what the email is about. It's bold, powerful, and gives the donor a reason to continue reading. Headlines may not always be necessary; however, if you're running an email campaign that spans multiple emails, then a headline may help to keep the donor engaged in your emails at each point of the story.

9) **Body:** The body of nonprofit emails may be one of the most contentious components that comprises an email. This is the part that historically has gotten the direct mail treatment, using long paragraphs, red underlining of key sentences to draw attention, and what appear to be handwritten signatures. Let me tackle each of these. First, though I'm not in favor of long paragraphs in email and treating them like a direct mail letter, I

have seen a few case studies online saying that longer copy has beaten out shorter copy in fundraising emails. Personally, I have tested this and not found that to be the case. I recommend testing this for your organization and see what works best. Second, the usage of red fonts and underlining sentences to draw emphasis should never be done in email. Ever. This is because in the digital world, the underlining of words denotes a link to another web page. In this case, you have two options: 1) Only use underlines if the word(s) link somewhere, like a donation page; or 2) Use bolded fonts instead of underlined fonts. Bolded words are equal to underlined words in direct mail. Last, when it comes to handwritten signatures in the closing of emails, use at your discretion. This is another example where I've seen case studies online that show handwritten signatures have caused a lift in fundraising revenue. I've tested this in several nonprofits and have observed that it neither helps nor hurts fundraising activities. When it comes to the design of the email body, some organizations are moving beyond a traditional letter-style format. Some are breaking up chunks of copy into different blocks and separating paragraphs of the story with different graphical elements like icons or images to help support the story being told. You know what I'm going to say next, right? Yep, I'd recommend you test different designs and see which one works best for your donor base.

10) **Offer:** After you've stirred the emotion of donors by telling a compelling, authentic story, you leave them with an offer to help. Be specific on the action you want your donors to take and what the impact of that result will be. The offer is usually no longer than a few words or a sentence. It would look something like, "Today, your gift of $22 can help provide a backpack full of school supplies for a child in need." Inclusion of an offer is what tips the scales towards donors opening their pockets. Think about it, if you read a story about a child in need, it may stir your heart. If you hear a story of a child in need, then are asked

specifically for help, that often opens wallets. If your nonprofit is more advanced with email segmentation based on donor-giving levels, the email content can be the same, but the offer may vary. Your offer for $25+ donors may be between $10-$30. Your $500+ donors may be between $100-$200.

11) **Call to Action (CTA):** Your call to action within the email is a visual cue to activate giving. It's the next step in the psychological and emotional journey. You read about the need that is expressed, are presented an offer of how you can help, then given a shiny button to click for the payoff. Anecdotally, I'd say that 95% of all nonprofit call-to-action buttons say, "Donate" or "Donate Now." That's the easy, safe approach. I'd challenge you to test the copy on CTA buttons to see if there is a lift in revenue. If the email talks about filling a child's backpack with school supplies, then maybe the CTA button doesn't say, "Donate Now" – instead it may say, "Fill a Backpack." Try tying in the copy on your CTA specifically to the offer. Other examples of alternative CTAs that you might test include "Match My Gift," "Feed a Family," "Save 10 Dogs," "Help Fund a Scholarship," etc. Be creative.

12) **Footer/Contact Info:** Legally, you must include a physical mailing address for your organization. This can either be a street address or P.O. Box. Without this information on your emails, your nonprofit could be subject to lawsuits. I'd recommend putting this information in the footer of your emails. I would also put an Unsubscribe link in the footer as well. So, yes, we'd have an Unsubscribe link at the bottom and top of your emails. Remember, we want to make it easy for people to opt out of receiving emails so that the email file can be of higher quality (i.e., people that actually *want* your emails). I would not include any social media links or icons in the footer or anywhere else in fundraising emails because it can detract from the purpose of the email, which is raising money.

Fundraising Email Tips

As we've gone through the anatomy of a fundraising email, I've shared several tips that might increase incremental revenue for your organization. I'd like to share a few more that aren't necessarily based on design, but more based on digital marketing principles. The following are all items that I have personally tested with clients and in which I've seen positive results:

- **Multiple Donation Buttons:** Sometimes a donate button at the top of your email can be overlooked because it's perceived to be part of the header of a template. Also, human beings have short attention spans. If a donor reads your whole email, they may forget about a donate button at the top of it, even though visually they saw the button before they actually read the email. I'd recommend a minimum of two donation buttons, one at the top and one after the body of the email. This allows donors to donate without needing to read your email while, at the same time, providing a donation opportunity that flows easily as the next step after the donor reads a compelling appeal contained in the body.

- **Eliminate Distractions:** The only goal of a *fundraising* email is to generate financial donations from donors. Because of this, you should eliminate any unnecessary distractions that take donors away from a giving mindset. This means stripping away any links or icons that may detract from obtaining a gift. This includes social media links. Why in the world, when you're asking someone to donate to your organization, would you send them down the wormhole of liking your social media page? Best case scenario, the link gets ignored. Worst case scenario, they click the social media icon, go to Facebook, and end up spending 20 minutes catching up on what their friends are doing, then forget to come back and make a gift to your organization. Only place the required links that will comply with CAN-SPAM rules, which is an Unsubscribe link.

- **Create Urgency:** One of the triggers that gets people to take action in marketing is what's called a "limited-time offer" or LTO. You see this all the time in other industries, especially retail or food service. The challenge for nonprofits is how to take your services or campaigns and give the appearance of a limited-time offer. The need is not there for a limited time. It's ongoing, which is why your organization exists in the first place. Part of the reason Year-End campaigns are successful is because donors have a strict deadline of December 31 to make a gift to receive tax benefits. The same is true for Giving Tuesday, but this is a deadline created by clever marketing. Donors can give the Wednesday following Giving Tuesday and still make a difference; however, the day has been marketed and generally accepted as a giving day, so there is urgency artificially created. You can create artificial urgency with your campaigns in a similar fashion with language like, "Today is the last day to give to the food pantry." Another way to create urgency is through special matching gift offers, where you match gifts for a period of time (i.e., "matching gifts this week only").
- **Resend Email to Non-Openers:** One easy way to gain incremental revenue from email is to resend your fundraising emails to recipients that didn't open your initial email. Depending on your email platform, you may have to manually export the names of those that didn't open your email and create a new list for your resend. Also, you want to give recipients at least a few days before resending the email to non-openers, in order to give late openers a chance to see your email. When you resend the email, you may try sending it at a different time of day, changing the subject line, or testing some other variable to see what works best for your organization. To set expectations correctly, you can expect to see a decrease in open rates for the resend email. For example, I've seen organizations that had a 15% open rate on

the initial emails have a 3% open rate for resends. In my opinion, it's worth it because you also obtain gifts that you wouldn't have received otherwise without this resend. You do this 12 times a year, and it could be the difference in several thousand dollars.

Affirmation Email Tips

We spent a good amount of time talking about fundraising emails because this is a direct marketing tactic necessary to drive revenue that can support your organization's services. However, if the only time donors hear from you via email is with your hand out, then you've failed them miserably. They want to hear from your organization in other instances, not just when you need money. They want to know they make a difference and that your organization is being a good steward of the gifts in which they've entrusted to you. Affirmation emails are a way to affirm their choice of supporting your nonprofit.

How do you measure the success of an affirmation email? The easiest way is to look at metrics like open rates, click-through rates, and unsubscribe rates. If you're able to look at a more granular 360-degree view of your donor through the CRM you're using, then you may look at engagement rates amongst different donor segments. For example, if your $500-$1,000 donor segment experienced a higher open and click-through rate on an email, then this may help to identify the type of content they engage with more frequently. This, in turn, could help your team provide more of this type of engaging content based on donor segment responses.

Outside of email metrics, if I'm a nonprofit, then I want my affirmation emails to be memorable and add something of value to the donor's life. Every time my donors get an affirmation email, it should strengthen their affinity for my nonprofit. The following are tips and ideas for affirmation emails. I've tested some of these, but others I have not.

- **Affirmation is Your Sandbox:** With fundraising emails, you don't want to stray too far from what works, unless you test another version first. With affirmation emails, I believe this is your sandbox and testing ground to see what donors latch on to. Try new designs, image effects, and types of content. Though there is less risk of harming revenue with affirmation emails, you still want to fall in line with your brand standards.
- **Links are OK:** I've banned you from using social media icons and links for fundraising emails, but it's totally OK for affirmation emails. In fact, you might even send out an email inviting people to join you on your social networks. Provide a benefit like unique content or a higher frequency of updates on your social media pages. You still don't want to go crazy by adding too many links, but it's okay to have an affirmation email template with social media and other icons and links.
- **Newsletter Block Format:** One of the coolest affirmation emails that I saw was a monthly newsletter email with a block-style format, similar to a website page. In this format, there was an introduction of the newsletter, followed by three different content blocks. Each block included the image of a person, along with a quote from that person, then a CTA button that said, "Read His/Her Story." The button pointed to a page on the website, similar to a blog, that captured the full story of this person whose life was changed by the organization. It was a beautifully designed and engaging email. The challenge with consistently doing an email like this is the lack of time most nonprofits have available to procure and produce stories for its website to which this email would point. My advice would be to start out small with a similar style but do it once or twice a year. I'd also include a CTA button for donations at the end of the story on the blog page.

This keeps the email as an affirmation, but also allows an easy way for donors to easily give for those that read the story and want to make an immediate difference.

- **Popular Affirmation Emails:** Affirmation emails come in many forms and convey different types of information. Here are some of the more popular types, some of which you may already be using:
  - *E-Newsletter Series:* Many organizations send a monthly electronic newsletter (e-newsletter) that contains updates or stories about the organization. This is a great way to keep your mission in the eye of your donors. You might also give your email series a name, rather than just calling it an "e-newsletter." Think of it like a magazine subscription. What would you call your organization's magazine? You might even test your email subject line when you send it to see if using the word "E-Newsletter" or the name of your e-newsletter in the subject line increases the open rate.
  - *Donor Affirmations:* Donor affirmations come in a couple of forms. One is an immediate email after somebody makes a donation to your organization. This thanks people in a timely fashion for their contribution and expresses gratitude along with how their gift will be used. Another form is after the conclusion of a campaign to report out results. For example, sending an email a few days after Giving Tuesday can let your donors know how much money was generated, how it will help, and to thank them for being a part of it.
  - *Event Announcements:* If you have an event coming up, whether online or in person, email is a great way to directly engage with your donors. You might even have exclusive events for a specific tier of donors, so

these emails can affirm their "VIP" status with your organization.

- o *Holiday E-Cards:* E-cards are an easy way to let donors know you are thinking about them during certain holidays or even for their birthdays. These should be fun, engaging, and relevant to your organization. You can use animation with e-cards and, in some instances, allow donors to forward or send e-cards of their own. It's a great way to keep your brand in front of donors on non-fundraising occasions.
- o *Story of Impact:* Every donor wants to hear a good story of how a life was changed, and how they were a part of this change. You can create a series (monthly, quarterly, etc.) and highlight a story of impact that an organization has made. This may be human, animal, something environment-related, or other type of impact your organization makes in the world. These are the feel-good stories that aren't asking donors for money. It affirms that the donor's choice of giving to your organization is a good one.
- **Affirmations Can Raise Money:** Though the primary goal of affirmation emails is not to raise money, they often do. In fact, in some cases, I've seen affirmation emails raise more money than fundraising emails. This is why I believe it is okay to keep a donate button at the top of your emails. I would recommend against using multiple donate buttons because, at that point, it could come off as offensive. You are a nonprofit and it is okay to provide an easy means for those that wish to donate via your affirmation emails. Don't feel guilty about it.

6

Email, Part 2

CAN-SPAM Overview & Email Blacklisting

According to the Federal Trade Commission website, CAN-SPAM is "a law that sets rules for commercial email, establishes requirements for commercial message, gives recipients the right to have you stop emailing them, and spells out tough penalties for violations." As a digital fundraiser, it's very important to be familiar with the CAN-SPAM Act. In fact, your organization can be subject to penalties of up to $41,484 per email that is in violation of the act. Please review https://www.ftc.gov/tips-advice/business-center/guidance/can-spam-act-compliance-guide-business to get a better understanding of the law.

As displayed on the FTC CAN-SPAM page, these are the main requirements:

1. **Don't use false or misleading header information.** Your "From," "To," "Reply-To," and routing information – including the originating domain name and email address – must be accurate and identify the person or business who initiated the message.

2. **Don't use deceptive subject lines.** The subject line must accurately reflect the content of the message.

3. **Identify the message as an ad.** The law gives you a lot of leeway on how to do this, but you must disclose clearly and conspicuously that your message is an advertisement.

4. **Tell recipients where you're located.** Your message must include your valid physical postal address. This can be your current street address, a post office box you've registered with the U.S. Postal Service, or a private mailbox you've registered with a commercial mail receiving agency established under Postal Service regulations.

5. **Tell recipients how to opt out of receiving future emails from you.** Your message must include a clear and conspicuous explanation of how the recipient can opt out of getting emails from you in the future. Craft the notice in a way that's easy for an ordinary person to recognize, read, and understand. Creative use of type size, color, and location can improve clarity. Give a return email address or another easy internet-based way to allow people to communicate their choice to you. You may create a menu to allow a recipient to opt out of certain types of messages, but you must include the option to stop all commercial messages from you. Make sure your spam filter doesn't block these opt-out requests.

6. **Honor opt-out requests promptly.** Any opt-out mechanism you offer must be able to process opt-out requests for at least 30 days after you send your message. You must honor a recipient's opt-out request within 10 business days. You can't charge a fee, require the recipient to give you any personally identifying information beyond an email address, or make the recipient take any step other than sending a reply email or visiting a single page on an internet website as a condition for honoring an opt-out request. Once people have told you they don't want to receive more messages from you, you can't sell or transfer their email addresses, even in the form of a mailing list. The only

exception is that you may transfer the addresses to a company you've hired to help you comply with the CAN-SPAM Act.

7. **Monitor what others are doing on your behalf.** The law makes clear that even if you hire another company to handle your email marketing, you can't contract away your legal responsibility to comply with the law. Both the company whose product is promoted in the message and the company that actually sends the message may be held legally responsible.

In addition to the legal ramifications of CAN-SPAM, you also need to be aware of the threats of being email blacklisted by email service providers (ESPs). A blacklist is a list containing blocked email addresses, domains, or IP addresses. You know what an email address is because you most certainly have one. A domain is whatever characters come after the @ symbol in an email. For example, the domain in the email address jeremy@MoreSpamPlease.com is MoreSpamPlease.com. An Internet Protocol address, or IP address, in general terms is the digital address of a computer. Similar to how you have a mailing address to receive a letter in the mail, you have an IP address so that other computers can connect to yours via the internet. If you're curious, you can find out your IP address by going to www.WhatIsMyIPAddress.com.

Email service providers like Gmail, Yahoo, Hotmail, and others have their own algorithms in place to weed out suspected spam emails from reaching the Inbox. Notice I said "suspected." I'd say that most email that is weeded out or goes to the Spam folder of your email is 100% spam. However, scenarios do exist in which ESPs will flag an email as spam, when it is not. Unfortunately, I've seen scenarios where nonprofits have been blacklisted, or what I call being thrown in "email jail." Just like the real world, it's easy to get into jail, but it's hard to get out. If your organization ends up in email jail, that means most, if not all, of your email subscribers will no longer get your emails in their Inbox. This means, less visibility, lower open rates, and less revenue generated via email.

Clearly ending up in email jail is not where you want to find your nonprofit's email communication. The following eight tips can help your emails avoid blacklisting:
Don't send image-only emails (this is a trigger for spam filters)
Include your nonprofit's address on every email (CAN-SPAM rule)
Include a clear email unsubscribe option (CAN-SPAM rule)
Honor email subscribers that unsubscribe and don't send them email (CAN-SPAM rule)
Send email from a dedicated IP address (not a pooled IP address, if you can avoid it)
Don't overuse red fonts (this is a trigger for spam filters)
Don't use "salesy" subject lines (this is a trigger for spam filters)
Follow the Golden Rule: Send the kind of emails that you would want to receive from a nonprofit

Email List Hygiene

Let's take a moment to talk about the importance of hygiene. I think we can all agree that personal hygiene is important. It keeps you healthy and prevents disease. As a bonus, when you have good hygiene, folks tend to stick around. If you have bad hygiene, people stop wanting to hang out with you as much.

Email hygiene functions the same. The process of cleansing the email records on your file are conducive to the health of your digital fundraising. In addition, poor email hygiene will result in the loss of donors hanging around. I briefly illustrated this when I introduced the Email section of this book. Recall the story where a majority of one of my client's emails that were being sent out around the holidays went to the SPAM and Bulk Items folders instead of the Inbox.

What I didn't tell you was that for some emails that were sent, up to 75% of the email addresses on file went to SPAM or Bulk Items folders. Grab your calculators and let's do some math behind this. Let's assume the email file size of this client was 40,000 email addresses, and they normally have an open rate of 10%. This means that about 4,000 people opened the email. If your fundraising email response rate is 0.06%, then that means you received 24 gifts. If your average email gift is $75, then that one email generated $1,800.

When we view this same set of numbers after 75% of emails went to the SPAM or Bulk Items folder, then it tells a different story. Now, instead of 40,000 email addresses, we're really looking at 10,000 email addresses that would have hit the Inbox. At a 10% open rate, this translates to 1,000 people opening the email. A 0.06% email response rate means that 6 gifts were generated for $450 total. If we look at the difference of $1,800 and $450, we're left with a difference of $1,350. If you sent one fundraising email a month under these conditions, then your organization may experience a $16,200 loss of revenue. This translates to thousands less meals served, nights of shelter, children sponsored, and more.

In the example I provided, it wasn't completely the nonprofit or the fundraising agency's fault. After all, up to that point, there was no penalty for an email file that didn't practice regular hygiene. Emails still hit the Inbox – money was still raised. Email hygiene was more of a "nice to have" rather than a "need to have." If I were in the shoes of a nonprofit Director of Development, I would've spent the few thousand dollars on digital fundraising tactics that would raise money, rather than that amount on email hygiene. Those days are now gone. It's now absolutely necessary for the existence of a successful digital program to utilize list hygiene.

My recommendation is to conduct email list hygiene at least once a year. I don't normally provide lists of vendors because companies can change names, go out of business, or be acquired by other companies. You can certainly search online for email hygiene service providers. Chances are, if you're currently doing list hygiene for direct mail with your organization, then that vendor can likely do email hygiene as well.

When conducting list hygiene, the following factors can be revealed about your email file:

- *The number of email addresses that no longer exist.* For example, if a donor used his or her work email address, but they no longer work for that company, then that email address would no longer be active.
- *The number of email addresses identified as SPAM email addresses.* This means the email hygiene service detected that a particular email address is associated with sending SPAM emails.
- *The number of inaccurate/undeliverable email addresses.* These may be emails that contain typos, which result in an email not being able to be delivered.
- *The number of inactive email addresses.* These are email addresses that may still be good email addresses; however, these emails are not experiencing any opens or clicks when they receive emails.

To set expectations correctly, when conducting proper email list hygiene, you will likely experience a large drop in the amount of email records on your file. I've had clients that lost 40%-70% of their complete email file due to email hygiene. Sounds like a bad thing, right? It's actually not. Remember it's about quality over quantity with your email file, which is why it's important to continually have email acquisition efforts going. Just like you need to replace donors due to attrition, you need to do the same with your email file. Another note to remember is that though your email file may have decreased 40%-70%, you can still use the entire 100% email file for digital advertising targeting on some social media platforms. So, all is not lost.

By now, you must be thinking, "How can I maintain the health of my email file so that my emails hit the Inbox?" This is a great question, so let me share the following tips:

1. **Create a plan and follow it.** Document how you will approach email hygiene, and make sure your team knows this plan. Don't sacrifice this plan, because sacrificing it may ultimately reduce the impact of your organization.

2. **Conduct a list cleansing 1-2 times a year.** Use a third-party vendor to cleanse your email lists. The end result is that they remove the low-quality email addresses, and you keep the high-quality ones. This means better opens, clicks, and conversions. It also means your reputation with email service providers like Gmail and Yahoo will improve.

3. **Remove non-openers from your file every 6 months to a year.** You have email addresses on your file right now of people that have not opened one email from you. Not one. Over time, the number of non-openers builds and degrades the health and reputation of your email file. Those non-openers are doing your overall file a disservice and should be removed after a period of time.

4. **Send "re-activation" emails to non-openers.** Before removing non-openers, you may conduct a "re-activation" campaign. You've probably seen something similar from email lists in which you subscribe. The subject line usually says something like, "Are You Still There?" or "This May be the Last Time You Hear from Us." Essentially, this is a last-ditch effort to engage email subscribers before you remove them from your list. To be clear, you should send this type of email *only* to subscribers you will potentially be removing from your list, not to your complete file.

5. **Implement an email Welcome series.** When someone signs up to subscribe to your emails or makes a gift to your organization, you should be sending a Welcome series via email. This series usually contains at least three emails, spread a 3-7 days apart. The first email should set expectations on how you will communicate with them via email and give new subscribers the opportunity to easily opt out. I've even said in the body of the email, "If you are not interested in receiving these types of emails, please opt out now." The second email may tell more about the organization and invite subscribers to follow them on social media channels or their blog. The third email may transition to an offer.

By following these tips, you are likely to experience a healthy, thriving email program that is hitting the Inbox of your donors.

Email Testing

Through the years, I've read tons of studies, blogs, and articles about what makes a successful email. Sometimes these are even broken down by industry to say that if you're in the nonprofit vertical, the best time to send an email is X time or X day of the week. These studies are helpful in order to understand the overall benchmark or pulse of what's working across an industry; however, approach with caution.

I imagine that if every nonprofit started reading these studies and adjusted their email approach accordingly, then we'd have a barrage of emails from nonprofits hitting our Inboxes at the same time and during the same day of the week. Naturally, this would lead to crowding in the Inbox, and the outliers that sent emails at another time or day of the week would be likely victors. A frequent question I get is "When is the best time or day to send an email?" Sure, there may be benchmarks, but my answer is always "Let's test it." If you can find nonprofit email benchmarks for time of day and day of the week, then I say try using those as your control. Unless, of course, you already have a control established for time of day and day of the week.

If you're not doing email testing, then now's the time to start. It's important because it helps you to better understand when your subscribers respond, which can lead to more revenue for your nonprofit. Otherwise, you're just throwing darts at a dartboard while blindfolded. It doesn't matter if you hit the target, so long as you hit *something*. This is not a sound approach.

Start with to defining *why* you want to test email. Documenting this reminds you that, though testing requires more time and effort, there is a purpose for doing it. You might say that the reason you're doing email testing is to determine which factors of the email execution help you raise more money. I'd challenge you to go a step further and look at the nonprofit's impact. The reason that you're testing email is to use technology to provide insight on ways you can provide more school supplies to children, fund more medical studies, sponsor more adults through drug rehab, etc.

After you define *why* you will conduct email testing, begin to put a plan together. For me, this starts out by making a list of all the things I'd like to know through email testing, which may include the following:
- What time of day will more subscribers open my emails?
- What day of the week will more subscribers open my emails?
- What kinds of subject lines result in higher open rates from my subscribers?
- What "From" name in my emails result in higher open rates from my subscribers?
- Does the placement or number of donation buttons in my email impact how many gifts are given?

- What kinds of images in my email result in a higher rate of donations?
- How do different email segments respond differently to the same email?
- Does the text contained on my donate button really impact how many donations I get?

If you're just starting email testing, keep it basic by conducting an A/B test as opposed to a multivariate test. An A/B test splits your email file into 2 groups, with each group getting a different version of the email. When conducting a test, it's a good rule of thumb to only change **one** variable. So, if you're testing what time of day results in higher open rates, then the only variable is what time of day the email is being sent. The day of the week, subject line, and content of the email is still the same between both emails. If you change multiple variables, then it becomes difficult to identify exactly which variable led to the difference in performance.

Email test plans that I've put together have always been done in Excel – and contain the following fields for both the Control and Test emails:
- Name of the email being tested
- Date of deployment
- Day of the week
- Time of day
- What is being tested?
- Test split (usually 50%/50%)
- KPI to determine test winner
- Which email won (control or test)?
- Statistically significant?
- Size of email file for each group tested
- Email open rates for each group tested
- Email CTR for each group

- Gifts for each group
- Total revenue for each group
- Average gift for each group

I usually lay it out like this in Excel:

	Email Tested	Control /Test	Date Deployed	Day of Week Deployed	Time of Day Deployed	What was Tested	Test split	KPI to determine which winner	Which Won?	Size of test (email send size)	Email Open Rate	Email CTR	Gifts	Revenue	Avg Gift
1	Email 1	Control					50%								
		Test					50%								

My approach is to start by testing items that will impact open rates. This is because the content of your email won't matter if no one opens it in the first place. So start with time of day, day of the week, subject line, and "From" name testing.

Plan out several tests ahead of time. For day of the week testing, it may look like this:
- Test 1: Tuesday vs. Thursday
- Test 2: Winner of Test 1 vs. Monday
- Test 3: Winner of Test 2 vs. Wednesday
- Test 4: Winner of Test 3 vs. Friday
- And so on, until you land on which day is achieving the highest metric in the goal you are measuring

As you can imagine, testing takes a lot of time. In the example above, just for day of the week testing, you're looking at potentially 5-6 email sends before you land on the optimal day of the week. If you only send 1-3 emails a month, then this may take months to complete.

Upon completion of the email test, you will want to determine if the results are statistically significant. This means that the control and variable populations and response rates were large enough to prove a clear winner in your test. If you don't know how to do this, then you can actually search online for email statistically significant calculators. There are many sites where all you have to do is plug in email metrics like open rates and sample size to get an idea of statistical significance.

I don't typically recommend email testing during November and December for fundraising emails. This is because a large amount of revenue may be at stake for your organization during this time of year. My advice is to test January through October and take the learnings from that timeframe and implement changes for your November and December emails.

Email Design Tips

The last section that we'll talk about when it comes to email is design. Once people click on your email, it's showtime, and the design can make or break whether the donor takes further action to make a donation. Email design best practices continue to evolve based on studies and user behavior; however, there are some facets of design that remain pretty consistent. The following are email design tips that can help your fundraising emails generate better click-throughs once you have the donor's attention:

- **Design for mobile first.** We've crossed the threshold where more than 50% of email is being opened up on a mobile device. The design of your emails should cater to mobile devices simply because, if it looks good on a mobile device, it will look great on a desktop computer. You don't want your potential donors to have to pinch the screen of their phone to zoom in just to read the email text. You'll lose your donor by doing this, along with their gift.
- **Use single-column design.** This tip relates to designing for mobile-first, but also falls into the evolution of email and website design. It used to be more popular to have two and sometimes three columns that would contain a picture or callout; however, those days are behind us. As general website and email design evolved to provide a better user experience, the elimination of multiple columns in email also

occurred. People are now used to scrolling on devices when they read email, and it makes all of the content more easily visible when images and email body copy are all in one column.

- **Centering headlines is OK but left align email body copy.** This falls under user experience (UX). As one creative director passionately told me, *"People don't read center aligned!"* He had a point. It's just a bad experience because your eyes have to constantly readjust at the starting point of the next line. Left-aligned body copy allows the eyes to easily and naturally reset to the same location as the previous line. Centering headlines is fine, but center-aligned body copy is not cute and falls into the triage of poor design.

- **Add a donate button on all emails.** This is my controversial tip, but I will keep it in here. I've tested donate buttons versus no donate buttons on affirmations, and there was no statistically significant difference in the performance of the emails. My recommendation is to keep the button on your emails if it's not hurting your response rates. Prove me wrong on this, and I'm willing to listen.

- **Personalize email with conditional content when possible.** If you're involved with direct mail, then you know that personalization within appeals can lift response rates. It's the same with digital. You can utilize conditional content, such as name, city, gift amount, and more in order to make your communication feel more one-to-one with the donor as opposed to one-size-fits-all messaging. Personally, an email would have more of an impact on me if it said, "Hello Jeremy, your gift of $50 is helping to make a difference in Atlanta," as opposed to, "Hello friend, your gift is making a difference in the community." It's the little touches that make a big difference.

7

Social Media

I conducted a webinar once and credited musicians for turning social media into what it is today. Going back to the origins of social media, online communities like Friendster (launched in 2002) were created as a way to keep friends connected, and also meet new people. MySpace then arrived and completely advanced the game in 2003 because users of the community could customize profiles, and musicians could share their music on the platform. Before it was called "social media," musicians created content in the form of songs, blog posts, and direct messages for fans and potential fans as a way to grow their fanbase. Musicians had to continue to post new content to continue engaging with their audience. Sound familiar? Keep in mind that musicians on MySpace were doing this organically without any advertising on the site. Also, corporations and brands were not on these sites and were slow to adapt.

In a sense, musicians created the blueprint for how to be effective in marketing at what would soon become known as social media. The same strategies and tactics applied by musicians on MySpace are the same exact strategies and tactics used today and considered best practices by corporations, brands, and nonprofits. Overstating the simplicity of how to be successful in social media, it can be boiled down to these ingredients: create authentic content (quality over quantity), engage with your audience, listen to your audience, and make your audience feel like they make a difference in who you are or what you are offering. That's it. This sounds a lot like what you do in fundraising, doesn't it? This is why I believe that social media and nonprofits are two peas in a pod. It just takes a little bit of time to strategize and plan out how to make social media work for your organization.

Just a quick tip, fundraising should *not* be the main goal of your social media plan. If the reason your nonprofit is active in social media is strictly to raise money, then you will waste a lot of resources chasing that rainbow with little to show for it. You can certainly raise funds through social media, and have a plan to do so; however, your main goal with social media should be to build relationships with your donors and potential donors. Running an effective social media strategy takes time to build and maintain, often without seeing a quick return on investment. In fact, I would not measure the success of social media by how much money was raised. Rather, I would look at audience size, audience engagement and, at a deeper level, how many of your digital and direct mail donors are active with your nonprofit on social media sites. Social media is a platform to build awareness, engagement, and advocacy. That being said, fundraising takes a back seat; however, it's still in the car and should be a part of your social media plan.

When it comes to social media, I usually identify three different categories of organizations: the *Intimidated*, the *Wannabe*, and the *All-In*. I believe the nonprofit's overall culture and leadership will determine the category in which they fall. The *Intimidated* are organizations that don't understand social media, so they don't even try. Social media seems too complicated or technical, and there's no true champion in the organization to help change this mindset. The *Wannabe* organizations really "wanna be" great at social media but lack the resources. These are the nonprofits that understand the value of social media and have likely even attempted to create a strategy and calendar to post content. However, the effort behind its social media is unsustainable because the person in charge of social media is also in charge of all digital marketing, or even all fundraising efforts, period. The *All-In* group of nonprofits not only understands social media, it also has at least one person on staff exclusively assigned to social media. These organizations have a sound strategy and are usually active on many social media sites. They regularly test content, build stories, respond to posts in a timely fashion, and create conversations. From what I've personally observed, most nonprofits fall into the *Wannabe* category, and few fall into the *Intimidated* or *All-In*. Which category best describes your nonprofit?

One of the fallacies that I have seen with the *All-In* nonprofits is that sometimes the social media strategy can be of such importance and priority that less attention is given to actual digital fundraising strategy. Social media is not a replacement for email, SEM, and website content, and should not be treated as such. A great social media strategy is one that falls into the nonprofit's overall marketing and fundraising strategy. Ideally, there will be a story arc that covers all marketing efforts. The way this story is executed through social media can be different and more rich through social media as opposed to other channels.

The following chart shows how many total active users are on the associated seven social media channels, along with what percentage of ages 50+ are active on each site. This data comes from Statista.com and the Pew Research Center. Notice that while Facebook has the most active users, YouTube edges out the number one spot for usage by ages 50+. An important item to keep in mind from a fundraising perspective is that the age of the average digital donor is 64, according to Blackbaud.

	Active Users	Usage for Age 50+
Facebook	2.2B	55%
YouTube	1.5B	56%
Instagram	813M	21%
Twitter	330M	16%
LinkedIn	260M	14%
Snapchat	255M	9%

This chart gives a clear indication as to why Facebook is naturally the first social media site that nonprofits flock to when it comes to establishing a social media presence. I'm a believer in "fishing where there are fish," and there are plenty of fish on Facebook. It's important to understand the similarities and differences between these channels. Let's take a high-level look at these six social media channels, along with pros and cons of each. For right now, we'll just look at these as social media platforms – I'll talk about the advertising capabilities of these a bit later.

Facebook
Year Launched: 2004

Description: Facebook started initially as TheFacebook.com and was really set up as an online community platform for colleges and universities. It was the first popular social media site that required you to use your real name on your profile. In its early days, you couldn't even have an account on Facebook without a .edu email address. Well, times changed and the business model evolved to be a profitable, publicly-traded business. As you can imagine, with over 2 billion members, Facebook has access to a level of personal data never so easily volunteered before by consumers. They know who you are friends with, what interests you have, where you live, where you work, who your family members are, and what kind of content you like to see. Every time you click on something in Facebook, you feed its data machine. Scared yet? As a consumer, it scares the crap out of me. As a marketer, I absolutely love it.

Pros:

- *Large donor audience:* Due to Facebook's sheer size, a large chunk of your donors are also on Facebook. In fact, the Baby Boomer generation is the fastest-growing generation on Facebook, so you will continue to see a trend in the increasing size of your donor base with Facebook accounts.
- *Various types of content:* Facebook is very diverse in the types of content that can be published including links to websites, images, videos, status updates, and live content.
- *Events:* Facebook allows you to post events, which can be great if you're trying to build awareness for a 5K, gala, luncheon, or other event.
- *Great analytics:* Facebook Insights is Facebook's analytics for its pages. There's a lot of great data to mine from Insights, including how many people engaged with each post, what time of day your audience is online, and what types of content get the best response. As far a social media sites are concerned, Facebook's analytics are ahead of the rest.
- *Tools for nonprofits:* A unique feature that also sets Facebook apart from other social media sites is that it has tools exclusively available for nonprofits. This includes the ability to add a donate button to your page and enable peer-to-peer fundraising. See www.nonprofits.fb.com for more information about Facebook's nonprofit features.

Cons:

- *Limited reach with organic posts.* Several years ago, a nonprofit could post content on Facebook, and a large chunk of its audience would see the post. There was a time when nonprofits would spend big money on Facebook advertising to attract followers (Page Likes) because the larger the audience, the more people it could reach. This is not the case anymore. Over time, Facebook updated how content shows up in your newsfeed. Even if nonprofits brought thousands of followers to its pages, a very small amount, maybe 2%-10%, of the people that liked its page would see the content on any given post. Which brings us to our next con.

- *Pay to play for more exposure.* Due to the dwindling of size of the audience that actually sees a nonprofit's post, it is now necessary to advertise or "boost" posts on Facebook if you really want people to see it. One of the great perks about Facebook for nonprofits early on was that it was essentially a free site to interact with the community, donors, and those that needed services. A large audience was built into the platform because Facebook was so massive. It was perfect for nonprofits where financial resources were sparse and every dollar counted. Well, now social media is no longer a free marketing channel for nonprofits if any impact is to be expected. It is now a channel that will require some fuel on the fire, i.e., advertising budgets, in order to make a difference.

- *Younger audiences abandoning the site.* When Facebook started, it was a younger generation's site. As the business model moved away from college students and more towards everybody, the floodgates opened up. The younger college students who ruled Facebook were now getting friend invites from their parents and grandparents. This meant older teenagers and younger twenty-somethings had to now filter themselves, their images, and posts or risk getting a good scorn by mom. I can only imagine how many young adults heard at least one of their parents say, "Do you have to talk like that and post those kinds of pictures? I raised you better than that." Needless to say, the younger audience is still a large population on Facebook, but many have jumped ship for other social platforms like Snapchat and Instagram.

- *Ever-changing algorithm.* The only thing you can predict about Facebook is that its algorithm will change. What that means to nonprofits is that what works today may not work tomorrow when it comes to reaching your donors. You can never be on cruise control in a set-it-and-forget-it frame of mind. Some changes are minor, but some can completely kill your nonprofit's visibility when it comes to what your page posts. A good place to check periodically for updates is direct from the source, Facebook's Newsroom (https://newsroom.fb.com/news/).

YouTube
Year Launched: 2005

Description: I remember when YouTube first started to really catch on. Droves of people were already on Facebook, which started to be referenced by some as "Crackbook," associating the site's addiction to the narcotic. Nevertheless, I was at a coffee shop one day and happened to run into a friend I hadn't seen in a while. His face was stuck – engaged with his cellphone as if his life depended on it. Though this behavior is commonplace today, it was abnormal in 2005. I asked him what he was looking at. He said, "Man, this is my new addiction. Have you heard of YouTube? They've got all these crazy videos on the site. I can watch it for hours." I actually had heard of YouTube, and had watched several videos myself, but I hadn't seen anyone as captivated with it like he was. This was definitely a sign of things to come, and a new wave to easily distribute and consume content. YouTube has continued to stay relevant and popular because the user base is so large, and pre-produced and live video content is still one of the most highly engaging ways to connect with an audience. YouTube is a Google product. The birth of Google's success was its simple focus on one thing, a search engine that only featured a search box on the page – unlike Yahoo, which featured a search bar along with news articles. YouTube didn't start out as a Google company; however, its focus on one thing – video – was a great fit with the Google ideology and business model.

Pros:

- *Video and livestreaming content.* No other website can boast of housing more video content than YouTube. In addition, as livestreaming has become more popular, Google added that feature as well. If content is King, then video is the King's daddy. It's at the top of the content food chain, and highly successful for nonprofits when it comes to storytelling.
- *Tools available for nonprofits.* Google for Nonprofits is a fantastic program for nonprofit organizations. I'll go into more detail about this program later in the book, but for YouTube, there are a few unique benefits available. Your nonprofit can put a donate button on its videos (USA only), have access to its own dedicated technical support, and use YouTube's production facilities in New York City or Los Angeles at no charge. This allows your nonprofit to not only make powerful videos, but also inject donate calls to action within your videos to capitalize on the emotion of a great video.
- *Ability to embed links in video.* A feature that I don't believe is used enough by nonprofits is the ability to embed links and pop-ups in videos. In addition to adding a Donate Now link to your video, imagine putting links in videos during relevant scenes of the story. You could really do a "Choose Your Own Adventure" style of video campaign by telling part of the story in video, then allowing users to choose (click a link) for what happens next in the video. That video could link to another video that continues the story, based on which link you select. In addition, organizations can use embedded links

in videos that point to volunteer and email sign-up pages. There's so many possibilities!

- *Most-used channel for donor age.* Going back to the study by Pew Research, YouTube edged out Facebook as the social media platform used by a higher percent of ages 50+. This means it's a great channel to reach prospective donors. With YouTube's ability to easily share and comment on videos, it's a great way to spread the impact of video content associated with fundraising campaigns.
- *Great analytics.* One of Google's strengths is its Google Analytics service provided for free to anyone with a website. Google also uses a robust set of metrics for the analytics provided within YouTube. You can learn the average time watched for your videos, traffic sources for your video plays, how many times people shared your videos, and more.

Cons:

- *Creating video is time-consuming.* Aside from a handful of videos that break out and become widely popular with little planning, most video creation takes time. In the nonprofit world, which is one full of great stories of impact, generally few resources are devoted to creating video content. Usually the person in charge of doing video content is also wearing 10 other hats, and whatever fire is burning that day will get priority. Video content takes planning, story gathering, interviews, writers, photographers, videographers, directors (or someone in charge of the project), editors, and more. In some nonprofits on a shoestring budget, these are all done by the same person. And that person might also be in charge of other day-to-day tasks within the organization not even related to video. I get it. This is a big challenge.
- *Video can be expensive.* Let's say you go the external route with your nonprofit and have an agency or freelancer create

and produce your video. If you can't be lucky enough to have it done pro bono by playing your "I'm a nonprofit" card, then you're likely looking at paying several thousand dollars for a video. The range can vary quite a bit, as I've seen as little as $2,000 and as high as tens of thousands of dollars. If you decide to take video in-house, then you still may be looking at purchasing or renting equipment, which won't come cheap. From my experience, I believe that price, more so than lack of resources, is the top reason more nonprofits don't have more video content available.

- *Nonprofit features require approval.* YouTube's nonprofit features are great, but not every nonprofit will qualify for them. You still have to go through the Google for Nonprofits process to be selected. In the event your organization is not accepted into the program, you can still be very effective with utilizing YouTube for your marketing and fundraising; you just won't have access to some of the key fundraising features. So, whether you're accepted into Google for Nonprofits, have little to no resources, or little to no budget, you still need to get in the game when it comes to video. Make it a priority for your next year's budget.

Instagram
Year Launched: 2010

Description: When Instagram was first introduced and some buzz started around it, I kind of dismissed it. I thought, "not another social media app to keep up with!" I went ahead and downloaded it, but it sat on my phone for months before I used it. When I actually started using it, I loved the different filters that were available on it. They would make the pictures from my phone look amazing, like I was a real photography pro. I didn't anticipate Instagram catching on like it did, but it makes sense. Images are powerful, and now everybody armed with a smartphone can look like a photojournalist. In the beginning, Instagram only offered images, but video capabilities were eventually added. This became important to keep up with other social networks that also allowed the posting of images and video. Instagram was purchased by Facebook due to its popularity and deep user base. Instagram continues to evolve quickly in order to keep up with competing apps, mainly Snapchat. If your nonprofit is using Instagram, remember, it's about the quality of the image, not the quantity. That's what gets the loves, shares, and comments.

Pros:
- *Images, video, and livestreaming features.* Instagram still relies on images as its base content but has branched out into other forms of content including video and livestreaming. This has helped Instagram retain its user base by staying competitive and offering many visual features that are available on emerging apps. Similar to stories, live video will be available on your Instagram profile for only 24 hours unless you save it to your highlights.
- *Stories that track multiple pieces of content.* Stories is a feature that allows users to add video and images in sequence over a 24-hour period. After that, the stories disappear unless you save them as a highlight on your profile; where they remain visible until you remove them. Combining stories with highlights are a great way for nonprofits to use original content to tell stories about their organizations or generate excitement at live events.
- *Advanced photo-editing features.* The array of filters available on Instagram is a huge part of what led to mass adoption of the app in the first place. Want your picture to look like it was taken in the 1970s? There's a filter for that. Want to give your picture a classic black and white look? Just slide to that filter and presto. No fancy editing skills or photo-processing skills needed. There are other apps available that provide filters for images; however, the simplicity and popularity of Instagram's

features make it one that nonprofits can use to effectively tell visual stories that make an impact.

- *Use of hashtags for tracking of topics.* Hashtags in social media were made popular through Twitter. The use of hashtags allowed users to easily find content related to those hashtags, and eventually became known as "trending topics." Marketers and fundraisers can utilize hashtags for branding and campaign purposes. With Instagram, like other social media platforms, this can bring awareness to the organization or campaign, while analytics tools can reveal how many times your hashtags were used in social media.
- *Owned by Facebook, evolving features.* Because Instagram is owned by Facebook, it has deep pockets to invest in the platform to stay competitive. This means advancing features to ward off competing social media sites and apps. In addition, it's easy to share content across both Facebook and Instagram once you connect the accounts to one another.

Cons:

- *Rate of changes makes app less intuitive.* Instagram remained relatively unchanged for years, with a focus only on images. The addition of video capabilities didn't change the platform too much either. The main threat to Instagram became Snapchat. As Instagram continued to add features to compete with Snapchat's offering, the interface of the app changed a bit, making it less intuitive. It still has a relatively easy-to-use interface; however, the newer features may not be as easy to figure out for users that have been used to Instagram's functionality for years.
- *Low donor demographic but growing.* Though Instagram is the third most-used social media platform behind YouTube and Facebook for ages 50+, only 20% of this age group are active on the app. This number likely skews differently depending on the organization. For nonprofits, the question

to ask is how many of your ideal donors are using the platform? If the answer is "not many," then it may not make much sense to invest a lot of time and resources into Instagram yet. However, even if you don't invest, this is a platform to keep your eye on because it will likely have one of the highest growth rates for your donor audience, similar to how Facebook's popularity exploded for Baby Boomers.

- *Designed as mobile app, so desktop suffers.* Though Instagram is available on desktops, the range of features, including the ability to add new content, is restricted to only the mobile app. This makes it a little more challenging to manage if your nonprofit is active on the site. Users can still view, like, and comment on desktop computers, but content creators, such as nonprofits, still can't publish from a desktop.
- *Ever-changing algorithm.* Similar to Facebook, the algorithm of what gets posted in a user's feed is constantly being tweaked. Though I haven't seen evidence of how this has impacted brands and nonprofits, I'm willing to wager that the eventual business model will be one similar to Facebook in that you will have to rely more heavily on advertising if you want your posts to be seen on Instagram.
- *Limited analytics.* Currently, Instagram's analytics, called *Instagram Insights*, is only available to businesses and accounts with high levels of engagement. This means if your nonprofit is not set up as a business account, then you won't have access to any analytics native to Instagram. Sure, you can manually see how many likes and comments your posts get with an individual account, but Instagram Insights provides many more features such as reach, impressions, website clicks, and more.

Twitter
Year Launched: 2006

Description: Twitter started out as a social media channel where users could share and post 140-character messages to followers. It was a simplified way to connect with others in short message bursts. Within Twitter, you also have the ability to like, share, and comment on other posts (called tweets). Through the years, Twitter has also evolved its features to stay competitive with other social media sites. It has added the ability to share images, video, and livestreams. What makes Twitter unique from other social media sites is its ability to quickly spread news and ideas. In fact, because tweets are user-generated content, many cases now exist where breaking news stories happen on Twitter before being reported by news stations. An interesting example of this took place on the night that the United States conducted the covert raid to capture Osama bin Laden. A Twitter user tweeted, "Helicopter hovering above Abbottabad at 1AM (is a rare event)." A few minutes later, the raid occurred. For nonprofits, the speed of sharing information and use of hashtags to categorize trending topics were instrumental in 2014's Ice Bucket Challenge for ALS.

Pros:
- *Images, posts, videos, and livestreaming videos.* Twitter has been able to stay relevant by evolving its features without sacrificing its core experience. Visually, its focus has always been a timeline of posts, mostly text-based, and the graphic interface and usability have been relatively the same for years. The different types of content, such as videos and livestreaming, have given more depth to the platform.
- *Expanded character limit to 280 characters.* In 2017, Twitter expanded the character count to 280 characters, which allowed for longer form messages. I was personally excited about this because many times it was challenging to convey a complete thought or message in 140 characters. However, I do believe it helped me as a writer be more succinct in what I

wanted to communicate. This expanded character count is a win for nonprofits as well because it allows for more opportunity to share stories about your donors, services, and more.

- *High use of trending topics and hashtags.* Twitter was the first social media site to popularize the use of hashtags. What started out as an easy way to follow and categorize content became a part of pop culture. People now literally say the word "hashtag" as a humorous ode to the popular use on social media. Jimmy Fallon and Justin Timberlake did a comedy bit about the pop culture use of hashtags that generated over 32 million views on YouTube. One way that nonprofits can use hashtags outside of campaigns is to go to Twitter each day, throughout the day, and see what hashtags are trending. Your organization can create its own clever tweets using the trending hashtags, which may provide a way for your nonprofit to inject its voice into more conversations. Make sure your organization's messaging is authentic and on brand though; otherwise, your organization could be skewered on Twitter by other users.
- *Decent account analytics.* Twitters analytics are pretty solid and continue to improve. Aside from basic metrics like number of followers, shares, and mentions, it also shows your account's most popular tweets of the month, most popular new follower of the month (in terms of his or her follower size) demographics, education, and more. These analytics can help you better understand who comprises your Twitter audience and compare that to your donor demographics. It also helps you to understand what type of content resonates with your Twitter audience.
- *Create lists and accounts to follow.* A cool feature that I personally believe is underused on Twitter is the ability to create lists of accounts to follow. This is an easy way to group people together to access their tweets more easily and more

quickly. For example, you could create a list of your highest valued individual donors to better steward them. You could also create a list of competing organizations to keep tabs on their marketing efforts. The good thing about lists is that you have the option of making them private so others can't see your lists.

Cons:

- *Small percentage used by ideal donors.* Only 9% of people ages 50+ in the United States are active on Twitter. While that may scare you away from using Twitter, it's still a channel to consider. My advice is usually to test it out for a while and see what works. If your nonprofit is at all involved in disaster response, then Twitter is a great way to quickly spread info. Though your donor audience is the most valuable, it is not your only audience. You also have volunteers, advocates, government organizations, and the media that may be interested in following your organization on Twitter.
- *Less personal, more anonymity.* While Facebook requires you to use your real name (or the name you tell them is your real name), a name on Twitter can be anything you choose that doesn't exceed 15 characters. This can allow for more "trolling," or negative comments, because users can hide behind a generic name. It also adds an additional layer when getting to know your donors because you may have to get through a screen name before you get the person's real name.
- *Cluttered newsfeeds.* As you follow more people on Twitter, your newsfeed gets more cluttered. This is because Twitter shows every tweet from the people you follow from newest to oldest. You can imagine that if you follow 1,000 people and each tweeted once a day, then that would be 1,000 tweets you would have to sift through. As of the time of this writing,

Twitter has begun to slightly modify the newsfeed so that it isn't as cluttered; however, it's still quite cluttered. This is why it's also beneficial to create lists, to reduce this newsfeed clutter.

- *No features exclusive to nonprofits.* Twitter does not currently offer services exclusive to nonprofits.

LinkedIn
Year Launched: 2003

Description: LinkedIn is primarily a social media networking site for professionals. As it's evolved, it has also become a site to look for jobs, as well as a platform to learn and share professional skills and information. LinkedIn offers the ability to publish articles similar to blogging, share presentations with SlideShare.net, or learn new skills through LinkedIn Learning (or Lynda.com). As a nonprofit, I recommend LinkedIn to be used primarily as a PR arm of your marketing efforts. It's a great place to share press releases and other organizational information. It's not a great site for individual fundraising campaigns; however, there is certainly value in networking with other professionals that may be grant writers or responsible for corporate giving.

Pros:
- *Establishes authority for company.* I've been surprised at how many nonprofit clients I've worked with that didn't have a LinkedIn profile. The primary reason given is that nonprofits tend to focus on more donor-focused social media platforms like Facebook. At a bare minimum, I always recommend establishing and completely setting up a company page on LinkedIn. Even if your organization doesn't plan on being active on LinkedIn, just having a presence establishes credibility and authority for your nonprofit. You can further

establish authority in your nonprofit's vertical by posting original content and articles on your company page. This provides your nonprofit's voice and point of view on your specific cause.

- *Good platform to reach corporate donors and grant writers.* Because LinkedIn is made up of professionals and companies, it is a great resource for researching and connecting with corporate donors. On LinkedIn, you can only send messages to people that are connected to you; however, LinkedIn offers premium paid services that allow you to send messages to anybody. This comes in handy if you're not connected to people responsible for corporate giving but would like to expand your network. You can also like and comment on posts from these individuals. A key to success on LinkedIn is to develop relationships with potential donors before asking them for money. If your first message to a person you've never met is asking for money or to talk to them about corporate giving, then that's one of the quickest ways to not get a gift. Remember, behind the LinkedIn profile and image, these are people like you and me that get turned off by blatant salespeople. Build the relationship first, then secure the gift.

- *Allows users to see employees of organization and learn more about them.* Because your nonprofit is a company that relies on funding to provide services, LinkedIn gives potential donors and the general public an inside view of what types of employees make up your company. People can view who works at your nonprofit – if they have a LinkedIn profile as well. This may help potential donors understand the professional experience and background of the people employed by your nonprofit. In a sense, it humanizes your nonprofit's brand because you can see the employees behind the scenes that are working hard every day for the cause that the donors are supporting.

Cons:

- *Site is for professionals, so context should be considered when posting.* This bullet point is not so much a con as it is a tip. Some nonprofits use social media posting aggregators like Hootsuite, which have the ability to quickly post content across several major social media sites like Facebook, Twitter, and LinkedIn. While this is great because it saves time, I believe that each site should have its own unique message. This gives people a reason to follow each account. If you're just pushing the same content out on all sites, then what's the point following each site? Would you post a cute cat meme that relates to your nonprofit on LinkedIn? I hope not. Do that on Facebook or Instagram instead. Think of LinkedIn as the newspaper for your nonprofit. Report out news, press releases, and other information relevant to professionals and corporate donors. Posting those cute cat memes on LinkedIn could work adversely against your nonprofit's brand because the messaging is out of context with the audience.
- *Little use by target demographic.* Only 14% of people ages 50+ are active on LinkedIn. This is another reason why you wouldn't pursue individual donors as heavily on LinkedIn. I wouldn't shame you for testing this out, because sometimes you want to see what may work for your nonprofit; however, I wouldn't suggest you prioritize investing in LinkedIn over Facebook or search engine marketing, for that matter. I had a nonprofit client that wanted to use LinkedIn as a way to attract a corporate match for an upcoming fundraising campaign. This is a good example of how to use the site. Context matters.
- *Limited analytics.* LinkedIn's analytics are adequate, but not stellar. They will let you know how many impressions, clicks, and interactions you receive with each post. However, the interface and layout of the analytics are a bit clunky. For

being around as long as it has, I find that the analytics of LinkedIn are behind other social media sites.

- *No features exclusive to nonprofits.* As of the time of this writing, LinkedIn offers no exclusive services to nonprofit organizations.

Snapchat
Year Launched: 2011

Description: Snapchat gained a lot of notoriety in its early days for being a "sexting app" because users could send pictures to each other that would disappear after 10 seconds. So, unlike texting a picture to a phone that could live forever, this time-disposable image approach became a big draw that created the foundation of a younger user base. Over time though, features evolved to include fun "lenses" (the kind that makes it look like you're throwing up rainbows when you open your mouth), geo-filters that included cool graphics for landmarks on your pictures and videos, and media content. With Snapchat, users can quickly and easily take a picture or video, add a caption or graphic, and send it to friends through the app. It also offered "stories" before Instagram, where users can create a collection of images or video and feature it in the order it was taken in a 24-hour timeframe. Brands, media outlets, and social media influencers have created content in which users can subscribe, which has made it a powerful and engaging platform to share content. Unique to Snapchat, when compared to the other social media discussed in this book, is that its features and content are only experienced through the mobile app. In addition, Snapchat allows brands to enable subscriptions to content that may include a collection of videos and pictures.

Pros:

- *Images, video, and livestreaming.* Snapchat includes a lot of the same image and video features available on other social networks. Though Instagram has begun to integrate a lot of features available on Snapchat, Facebook seemingly has added even more. Facebook, in response to Snapchat, now includes stories, lenses, and the ability to add additional graphics to images.

- *Fun filters and lenses (some user-generated).* One of Snapchat's strengths is its use and popularity of "lenses." Though they weren't the first phone app to feature lenses, Snapchat really helped increase the popularity of lenses. It's just plain ol' fun to see a picture or video of yourself with dog ears and a tongue wagging, am I right? Though other social media platforms have added lenses, Snapchat has a strong focus on enhancing their own. If you have 2D or 3D animation skills, Snapchat will allow you to create your own lenses that you can share with others. What's cool about this for nonprofits is that you can partner with a graphic designer and create unique filters for your organization that can be shared with your organization's friends on Snapchat. This helps with branding and creates a way to engage with the next generation of donors at a younger age.

- *Younger donors rule the platform right now.* As a nonprofit, why should you use Snapchat if other social media platforms offer many of the same exact features? There are a few reasons, but the main one is because it contains a trove of future donors. Forty-five percent of Snapchats users are between 18-24 years old, and roughly 70% of the users are female. This is not a demographic that gets a lot of attention from nonprofits when it comes to fundraising, simply because they don't have much money to give. There is value to engaging with this demographic while they are younger and meeting them where they are, so that when they do have money to give, your organization will be top of mind. However, unless you're a unique nonprofit that acquires a majority of your individual gifts from this demographic, then I would not make Snapchat a priority when it comes to your social media strategy. I believe it's important to have a presence on Snapchat, but I also understand how restricted time and resources can be for nonprofits to successfully manage Snapchat.

Cons:

- *Tricky user interface (UI).* If you're a new user to Snapchat, you may find the app confusing or difficult to use because it's not very intuitive. Many people migrate from Facebook to Twitter to Instagram to Snapchat. It takes a little bit of patience to really understand Snapchat because the content is not presented in a timeline format like the other social media sites. Some features are also unique to Snapchat, so it provides a very different experience.
- *Smallest use by donor demographic.* At just 7% of people ages 50+ active on Snapchat, it is not the ideal channel to go fishing for donors. Adoption rates may increase over time, but I don't anticipate the active users in that age group being large enough to make an impact for some time. It's not a lost cause for your nonprofit though. There is certainly demographic research available that shows though younger generations, particularly Millennials, don't have a high net value, they do have influence on the older Baby Boomer and Silent generations. A unique relationship exists between these younger and older generations as many Millennials are the grandkids of those generations. This younger generation is really big into advocacy, but most don't have the money to support causes. This is where they can use their influence on older generations, which do have the money, to make a donation. And there's no better social media channel right now to reach Millennials and Generation Z than Snapchat. That said, think of Snapchat more as an influence channel, rather than a fundraising channel.

- *Heavy competition may suppress growth and adaption.* Snapchat certainly has its own features unique to its platform; however, other social media platforms are able to adopt some of Snapchat's more popular features relatively quickly. So the question I ask myself sometimes is whether or not the Snapchat user base will plateau soon. I'm thinking that if Facebook, Instagram, and even Twitter begin to utilize the most popular features of Snapchat, then maybe those users won't want to be active in yet another social media app. Will Snapchat remain a younger person's app, or will older folks migrate over and cause the younger generation to flee like they did on Facebook? That remains to be seen.
- *Removed ability to send money.* Snapchat used to have a feature available called Snapcash where users could send money to other Snapchat users within the app. This was completed through a partnership Snapchat had with Square; however, that ended in August of 2018. I was really excited about the possibilities of this feature for nonprofits, especially as it pertained to easily obtaining gifts from a much younger donor base. On the one hand, it provided a low-friction way for organizations to gain donations. On the other hand, it would be another revenue channel to keep up with, and I don't know whether or not nonprofits would have access to the donor data or not.
- *No features exclusive to nonprofits.* As of the time of this writing, Snapchat offers no exclusive services to nonprofit organizations.

One of the newer features available on most social media platforms is the ability to livestream video. Just like it sounds, this is video shot on the spot without any editing. Effective marketing is rooted in authenticity, and it doesn't get more authentic than a live video that may include mess-ups, stuttered speech, or anything else that would be less than an ideal, polished video. At the same time, the viewer of a live video gets to see a story or news unfold at the exact time it occurs, leaving a feeling of exclusivity.

I've seen a few nonprofits embrace live video, and it's really exciting when done right. Think about how you can use it for your organization – even for fundraising. Make it a goal this year to implement livestreaming at least once. Here's a short list of ideas to get your brain stirring:

- Major organization announcements like a new corporate sponsorship or celebrity endorsement (especially if the celebrity is live with you)
- Giving Tuesday "command center" that provides donation updates throughout the day
- 24-hour (or longer) fundraising marathon where your staff or organization is live until $X amount of money is raised
- Walkthroughs of hospitals, animal shelters, disaster relief warehouses, food kitchens, or other physical locations where services and impact take place (make sure you get consent from others before featuring on video)
- Exclusive interviews with organizational leadership or individuals helped by your services
- Use at live events such as a 5K, gala, or other event
- Once live video is recorded, most platforms allow you to save that video, which can become a great piece of content for your library

8

Digital Media

Digital media is pretty much any advertising that takes place through the internet, reaching desktops and mobile devices. It comes in many forms including search engine marketing, online display ads, social media ads, video ads, native ads, Inbox ads, and more. Digital media can be used to accomplish several different goals, depending on what your organization is looking to accomplish. For example, through digital media, you can generate awareness, drive traffic to your website, acquire email addresses, and increase online donations. Sounds great, right?

While there can certainly be a lot of good to come from investing in digital media, it is not a guaranteed money maker. I've worked with chapter-based organizations that utilized the exact same SEM program with the same keywords, ad copy, ad budgets, and during the same timeframe. Interestingly, some made a lot of money, some made a little money, and some lost money. To this day, I can't explain it. Perhaps the messaging of the ad didn't quite resonate in certain geographic locations, or maybe competing organizations were more popular in a specific geographic area and those organizations received more funds. Perhaps the geographic markets that lost money typically don't contain a concentrated number of donors. Either way, the key with digital media is to create tests with your ads until you find what works best for your organization.

Pros:

- The speed in which you can test ads in digital media is unmatched by any other form of fundraising. With direct mail, because the production process is so lengthy, you can only test one campaign at a time. Even then, you may not have the results back in time to adjust for the next mailing campaign. With digital, you can learn test results in a matter of days and make immediate adjustments.

- The targeting ability of digital media is quite robust and seems to be only getting better. In the early days of digital media, it was almost a one-size-fits-all type of targeting, with the exception of paid search, which relies on keywords. You now have the ability to target audiences by zip code, age, interests, device type, time of day, day of the week, email address (if your organization has it), web page visits, and lots more. Each ad platform has its own targeting abilities, so not every digital media platform can target based on the same factors. The only threat to the targeting ability may be privacy laws that restrict how online ads are targeted.

- Digital media is interactive by nature, meaning they were created for users to click – or interact with them. Though most display ads are only utilized to generate awareness, they are still designed for users to click and be taken to a web page. The use of images and animation in some ads also helps to draw attention and engage donors, unlike other forms of paid media.

- There are so many types of ads to reach donors through digital channels that it's almost scary. This is great for organizations because it literally allows you to reach your donors online wherever they visit. While they're checking email, you can serve them an ad that appears at the very top of their Inbox. If they are searching on Google for something related to your organization, they can be served an ad for your nonprofit. If they are checking their favorite news or finance sites, they can be served an ad. It's wonderful. And scary. But mostly wonderful.

- The barrier to entry for getting into digital media is extremely low, especially if you want a quick test. Unlike broadcast, which may take thousands of dollars in which to advertise, digital media can work with practically any budget. And I do mean any. I'll talk more about different ad types shortly, but if you have $100 and an hour to learn how to set up a Facebook ad, then you can get in the game. Even though this barrier to entry is low, the learning curve may be high, which is why many organizations still don't delve too much into digital media in-house.

Cons:
- If your nonprofit has never done it before, it's difficult to predict your organization's performance. Since you have no historical information to estimate ROI, you have to rely on industry sources. This helps a little bit, but usually organizational leadership wants to know, "If I spend X, will I get X in return?" I can't fault them for thinking that way because a good business mind should think like that, and it's based on a direct mail approach that has years of historical data. With digital, you may want to approach the first year as a test with no expectation of making money, and perhaps even losing some of your investment.
- Not all digital media channels make money. Historically, I've experienced with my clients (and supported by industry studies) that search engine marketing has a higher chance of making a positive return on investment. This is based on last-touch attribution, meaning that SEM was the last stop on the donor's journey before he or she made a gift. SEM is more a direct-response style of digital media, while social media ads and online display ads are more of an influence style of digital media. Influence, in this case, means that a donor was

influenced by a social media or online display ad, but didn't click on the ad to make a gift; however, this donor did make a gift through another fundraising channel. The donor was influenced on his or her giving journey by the online ads.

- The barrier of entry for digital media is limited by your budget. Can you get into the digital media game with $5? Sure, but you won't raise much money or learn much. What's the right amount you should budget, $5,000, $20,000, $50,000, more? Depending on your goals and nonprofit's resources, the answer is "It depends." I get the budget question all the time from clients, but I typically have to turn the tables back on them. If there's historical data of digital media performance, it can provide insight into donor acquisition costs and ROI. If not, then the question becomes more about what size budget are they comfortable with testing in digital media. Based on that number, it helps to identify which digital media channels make the most sense and how much to allocate for each channel.

- It can be a tricky maze to navigate if you've never done it before. With the large array of digital media channels, ad platforms, ad types, and ad specs, one could easily bury his or her head in the sand from feeling overwhelmed. The ability for a nonprofit to have a person or persons on staff to strategize, plan, execute, and measure digital media is a rarity. I find in most cases some of the work is done in-house, and the rest is done by an agency, freelancer, or consultant...which adds to the overall media cost.

Now that we've discussed some of the pros and cons of digital media, let's take a look at a few of the more popular digital media channels. I've identified three that are utilized the most by nonprofits from my experience, which include search engine marketing (SEM), online display ads, and social media ads. There are books available online if you're looking to get a deep understanding of each of these channels, as well as online training provided by both Google and Facebook. For the purpose of this book, I'd like to give you a broad overview of the capabilities and use cases of each type of these three digital media channels.

Search Engine Marketing (SEM)

What is it? Search engine marketing is the text-based advertising that appears in search results after people search specific words or phrases on search engines. I'll use Google Ads as an example because 75% of all web searches in the USA occur on Google. How it works is that you set up an account with Google Ads, select the keywords that you'd like to bid on that are relevant to your nonprofit or campaign, write copy for the ads, select budgets for your keyword, select your daily or campaign budget, then – voila – activate it. This is a simplified version of how it works, but it's enough to let you know there's no magic to it.

Because SEM is a pay-per-click, your organization is charged each time someone clicks on your ad and is charged at whatever amount won the bid for that keyword. For example, if you bid $5 per keyword, but others were bidding $4.25, then you would've won a placement of your ad by buying that keyword for $4.26. Google will show your ads high enough and often enough to come close to meeting your daily or campaign budgets.

For nonprofits, SEM is one of the top digital revenue streams, especially in Q4. Outside of Q4, I've seen mixed results in terms of providing positive ROI, so approach with caution. I've also noticed, and had validated by industry studies, that the average gift from SEM is larger than email. SEM is an important channel for fundraising and should be one of the first digital media channels added to your fundraising mix. SEM can also be used to drive people to volunteer or visit email sign-up pages; however, the cost per volunteer or email sign-up can get high. You'd want to keep tabs on how much you're spending on ads versus how many volunteer or email sign-ups you get to determine if it makes sense for your nonprofit.

Who is it? Google Ads is the most popular due to the sheer traffic on Google. Next is Bing Ads, which gets ad placements on Bing and Yahoo search engine results pages (SERPs). Some great items to note about Bing is that you can import your Google Ads campaigns directly into Bing for quick and easy set-up. This saves time from having to start from scratch when setting up ads in Bing. I've consistently noticed lower cost per click on Bing Ads for many of the same keywords on Google. This is because the search traffic is lower on Bing's search engine, and there aren't as many advertisers to compete with. Both Google Ads and Bing Ads have their own networks of smaller search engine sites in which they can also place your ads.

Why would you use it? You would use SEM as direct-response fundraising and competitive tactics. On average, 3.5 billion searches take place on Google every day. Donors are searching for your organization or other donation pages to which they can donate. You want to ensure your nonprofit has a presence on the search engine results page in order to drive prospective donors to your donation pages and acquire gifts. From a competitive standpoint, other nonprofits will bid on similar keywords as yours, and maybe even bid on your organization's name as a keyword. This means if someone searches for your organization by name on Google, then that competing organization may show up ahead of yours on the search results page. Bidding on your own brand name and related keywords helps to box out competitors, in a sense.

When would you use it? You would use SEM to coincide with your integrated fundraising campaigns, especially in November and December when fundraising heats up. Outside of Q4, you may want to test with fundraising campaigns.

What kind of results can I expect? In general, SEM ads generate a positive ROI. According to the 2018 M+R Benchmark Report, search ads had a $3.81 return on ad spend. This means that for every dollar invested in search ads, nonprofits gained $3.81 in return.

Types of targeting available: As of this writing, there are six buckets of targeting available on Google Ads, which are as follows (taken directly from Google's site):

- **Demographics:** Target your ads based on locations, ages, genders, and device types.
- **Affinity:** Nonprofits with TV campaigns can extend a campaign online and reach an audience using Google Search.
- **In-market:** Show ads to users who have been searching for services like yours. These users may be looking to make a donation or have previously made a donation and could still be interested enough to interact with your ads.
- **Custom intent:** Choose words or phrases related to the people that are most likely to engage with your site and make donations by using "custom intent audiences." In addition to keywords, custom intent audiences let you add URLs for websites, apps, or YouTube content related to your audience's interests.
- **Similar audiences:** Expand your audience by targeting users with interests related to the users in your organization's email lists. These users aren't searching for your organization or services directly, but their related interests may lead them to interacting with your ads.
- **Remarketing:** Target users that have already interacted with your ads or website so that they'll see your ads more often. These users can be in any stage of conversion, as long as they've visited your site or clicked on your ad before. These users may even return to complete a donation.

Important to note: If you're new to Google Ads, let me save you some money that you may otherwise be throwing away in low-quality ads. The following is a list of a few tips you should use as a foundation for your SEM ads:

- Capitalize all words in your ads. Yeah, I know that isn't proper, but this has proven to be a winner across the board and across industries. You can see an example of this in the ad below that I've used for my own online course.

> Digital Fundraising Blueprint | Self-Paced
> Online Course $499
> jeremyhaselwood.com/Digital/Fundraising
> For Nonprofit Professionals. 30-Day No Risk
> Guarantee. Learn More

- End your ad with a call to action (CTA). For nonprofits, this CTA will like be something like, "Donate Now," "Please Give," or something along those lines. Because your character counts are limited, you'll have to get creative with your CTA.
- Point ads to a landing/donation page, rather than a homepage. If you point ads to your homepage, rather than your donation page, you will get little to no results. This is because there are too many distractions on your homepage with many different places to click. It also may not be relevant to your ad. By pointing your ads directly to a donation page, your ad is relevant to the actual messaging on the page. This helps increase your donation conversion rate.
- Use copy that also appears on the landing page. Each ad has a quality score that figures into determining where your ad will place on search engine result pages. Part of this score looks at what your ad says versus what's contained on the landing page the ad points to. For example, if your organization's ad is talking about feeding the homeless, but your landing page

is talking about helping kids get to summer camp, then your ad will likely have a low-quality score. This may prevent your ad from running.

- Use URL parameters (UTMs) to track campaigns in Google Analytics. By using UTMs on your links, you can learn more about your campaign's effectiveness in Google Analytics. This is because Google Analytics will tell you how much traffic the ad generated, how long that traffic stayed on your site, how many abandoned the site, and even how many donations (or conversions) occurred. Learn more about this at https://ga-dev-tools.appspot.com/campaign-url-builder/.

Google Ad Grants

What is it? Google Ad Grants is a SEM service that's available after your organization is accepted into the Google for Nonprofits program. This program is available in 50 countries and offers *up to* $10,000 a month in free SEM advertising spend. Because it's a free service offered by Google, there are a few differences in the available features between Google Ads and Google Ad Grants. First, with Google Ads, your maximum bid on any keyword is capped at $2.00. This is why I recommend also setting up a Google Ads account in addition to Google Ad Grants because some keywords can rise above a $2.00 bid, especially around the holidays. Also, Google Ad Grants only allow for text-based ads, so you do not have the full suite of Google's available ad units like display, video, shopping, or Gmail ads. Your nonprofit's ads will only appear on Google's search results, not its partner sites, and will be featured in positions below paid advertisers. Even if you don't have someone on staff to set up and manage Google Ad Grants, it's worth partnering with an agency, freelancer, or consultant to manage this for you. Sure, that'll cost you money, but it also gains you access to the free advertising and expands your marketing and fundraising efforts.

Who is it? This is a service provided exclusively by Google. For more information, please visit https://www.google.com/nonprofits.

Why would you use it? Because you are given $120,000 of free advertising a year on Google search, you can get creative with how you use your Ad Grant. These would be my recommendations:

- **Campaign support** – Use your grant as a SEM channel for your integrated fundraising campaigns.
- **Awareness** – Drive awareness of your organization and services offered by using your grant and driving traffic to different pages within your website.
- **Reach people that need your help** – Create ads that cater specifically to people that may need your services. Drive this traffic to specific pages within your website that cater to people that need your organization's help.
- **Increase volunteers** – Create campaigns with your grant that point to a volunteer sign-up page on your site.
- **Increase email subscribers** – Create campaigns that drive traffic to your email sign-up page.
- **Fundraising** – Create evergreen/generic fundraising ads that run year-round.
- **Donate items** – If your organization participates in donating clothing, food, household items, or any other goods, you can use your grant to drive traffic to those pages on your website that let donors know how and where to donate.

When would you use it? To remain eligible for the Ad Grant, your organization will need to run ads year-round. A few other stipulations you need to know about remaining eligible are as follows:

- **Geo-targeting** – Your ads need to geo-target specific locations, as opposed to being set to show worldwide.

- **Ad groups** – Your account needs to have at least two different active ad groups per campaign, each containing a set of closely related keywords, along with two active ads.
- **Sitelink ad extensions** – Your ads need to utilize at least two sitelinks. These are links that usually appear at the bottom of your ad, in a different color font, that link to pages within your website. In the example below, there are four different sitelinks, starting with "More Ways To Give."

American Cancer Society® | Donate Now & Help Save Lives
Ad donate3.cancer.org/ ▾
Cancers, All Stages, Every Day. That's What We Do. Join The Fight Today. ACS Official Site.
Dedicated to Prevention. 100 Years of Progress. We Work to Find Cures. Give Now. Save Lives..
More Ways To Give · Donate by Mail or Phone · You Can Help Save Lives · Programs & Services

- **Click-through rate** – Your Ad Grant's account must maintain a 5% click-through rate (CTR) each month. If your account goes two months without meeting this threshold, then your it will be temporarily deactivated.
- **Conversion tracking** – In order for your Ad Grant to go live, you will need to have at least one conversion tracking goal set up in Google Analytics for your website. Conversion tracking reflects goals within your website such as donations, volunteer sign-ups, or email sign-ups. You can learn more information about Ad Grants conversion tracking here: https://support.google.com/grants/answer/9038650

What kind of results can I expect? I've worked with many clients that have obtained Google Ad Grants, but very few have actually reached the $10,000 monthly threshold. National organizations have a better shot at getting close to that amount versus local or regional organizations. If managed effectively, you can receive a lot of traffic to your site, which results in more brand awareness, engagement, and donations.

Important to note: Not every organization that applies will be accepted into Google for Nonprofits. Also, if you apply and get rejected, try again. I've seen cases where nonprofits get rejected, then reapply and get accepted. There are a few boxes to check before you submit your application, including the following:

- Register as a charitable organization through www.TechSoup.org
- Your nonprofit cannot be a government entity or organization, hospital or health care organization, school, academic institution, or university (but philanthropic arms of educational institutions are eligible)
- Determine if there are other detailed requirements for your country. Find out here: https://support.google.com/nonprofits/answer/3215869?hl=en&ref_topic=3247288

Online Display Ads

What is it? Online display ads are advertisements that appear on websites or mobile apps through banners that may contain images, text, video, or animation. The Interactive Advertising Bureau has worked to standardize 15 different sizes (in pixels) of display ads and names, which are as follows:

1. Vertical rectangle: 240 x 400
2. Mobile leaderboard: 320 x 50
3. Banner: 468 x 60
4. Leaderboard: 728 x 90
5. Square: 250 x 250
6. Small square: 200 x 200
7. Large rectangle: 336 x 280
8. Inline rectangle: 300 x 250
9. Skyscraper: 120 x 600
10. Wide skyscraper: 160 x 600
11. Half page: 300 x 600
12. Large leaderboard: 970x90

13. Large mobile banner: 320 x 100
14. Billboard: 970 x 250
15. Portrait: 300 x 1050

Display ad costs are usually based on cost-per-thousand impressions; however, they can also be based on cost per click or cost per conversion. According to Google's ad research, the most effective of these 14 ads are the large rectangle, medium rectangle, leaderboard, half page, and large mobile banner. In addition, animated ads typically perform better than static images.

Let's talk about how these ads work in simple terms. Basically, the internet has a large bucket of inventory on millions of websites where display ads can appear. Display ad providers and platforms can work with their customers (the nonprofits) to get their ads placed on these websites. The nonprofit sets a budget and provides creative to the ad platform or provider, along with any audience targeting information. Then, the display ad providers make sure your ads get seen on sites they deem relevant to your specifications. A benefit of display ads is that they can reach donors all over the internet, not just on search engines.

My personal preference for display ads when it comes to nonprofits is to primarily run them on desktops as opposed to mobile. While many more people have access to mobile devices, more donations are made through desktops. Also, display ads on mobile devices can sometimes burn through ad budgets more quickly because they tend to get clicked on more frequently than desktops. These clicks are usually unintentional, as people "fat finger" the ads, trying to close them or scroll past them on smartphones. I go with the philosophy that "the quickest path to the money," when it comes to display ads, is through desktops.

Who is it? Many companies provide access to display ad networks. Some companies, like Google, allow you to do more of a self-service style where you set up and manage your own campaigns. Other providers set up and manage everything for you through their own ad platforms. Because so many of these companies go through mergers and acquisitions, I won't list them in this book because it may be outdated by the time you read it. If you're just starting out, you may start with Google's display network because it can be easily managed with Google search ads as well.

Why would you use it? The main reason to use display ads is for generating awareness. If you are investing in display ads in hopes that your donations will skyrocket, then you will be sadly disappointed. So, why use display ads at all if they don't make money? A study came out several years ago that said, on average, a person sees a marketing message seven times before making a buying decision. Display ads would be one of those seven touches, but most likely the donation would still come through direct mail, email, or a SEM ad. Remember the philosophy of "fishing where there are fish." Your display ads will reach an audience of donors and potential donors that may or may not be getting your other marketing message. It's a way to extend your campaign or brand's reach. Display ads are the billboards of the internet, but with much more targeting and sophistication.

When would you use it? You would use display ads as a support to an integrated fundraising campaign. I would not recommend running display ads solely by themselves without other marketing channels. You certainly could do that, especially around the holidays. However, overall campaign performance will be stronger if you run display ads along with your other marketing mix. Retargeting existing donors or website visitors has proven to be the most successful use case of online display ads. In this case, your ads are shown to your donors or to people who have visited your website and not completed a donation. It reminds them to come back and complete their gift, and they are a "warm" audience.

What kind of results can I expect? Depending on your budget, you can expect a ton of impressions, a few clicks, and even fewer donations. Think of online display ads as that finger that taps your donors on the shoulder to say, "Hey, don't forget about me."

Important to note: Ad fraud has been one of the biggest issues when it comes to online display ads. The biggest problems are third parties overstating the amount of views and impressions your ads get by placing multiple sizes of your ad on one page and counting each size as an impression. Realistically, if three different sizes of ads appear on one page to one user, it should be one impression, not three. Also, some platforms and providers count (and charge) an ad as an impression, even if it is not visible to the person online. How this happens is that the ad may appear at the bottom of the page, but the person has not scrolled down the page to actually see the ad. If you're working with a third party to place ads for you, make sure you understand what counts as an impression and how impressions get counted.

Social Media Ads

What is it? Oftentimes, when I meet with nonprofits, they ask a lot of questions about social media. They say things like, "We need to get better at social media" or ask "What are some tips you can give me for social media?" Most of the time, they don't know what questions to ask or where to start, and that's okay. Social media is not simple, nor is it just about posting content in hopes that it will become viral. Nowadays, you can't talk about social media without having a discussion about social media advertising.

A quick tidbit of history for you. Not one of the popular social media sites started out with advertisers. They were communities where people could go, free from being commercialized, and simply connect with other people. It wasn't until the sites accumulated millions of users that they decided to monetize use of their platforms. Through the trove of data available about the users of their sites, social media companies now have the ability to target individuals in a way that never existed before. Want to target people who like peanut butter and jelly sandwiches? You can do that through Facebook Ads. It's crazy!

Social media advertising is becoming more important if you want your organization to reach an audience on these sites. This is due to the social media platform algorithms constantly changing, and restricting what messages get seen in users' feeds. You can't assume that if you have 10,000 friends or followers that they will actually see your organic posts. In some cases, as little as 2% of your audience will actually see your organic posts. This is why, unfortunately, social media is becoming a "pay-to-play" communication channel – if you really want your audience to see your messages.

Social media ad management functions similarly to SEM in that many are based on a cost-per-click or cost-per-thousand-impression basis. You can typically designate a daily budget or lifetime budget for campaigns as well. If you are comfortable managing and executing SEM ads, then the transition to social media ads is pretty intuitive because of these similarities.

Who is it? Advertising is available on all the social media sites we've reviewed up to this point. The audiences that you're able to target and the types of ads vary between platforms, so you'll have to decide what is best for your nonprofit, depending on your advertising goal. The following is a summary of each:
- Facebook
  - Advanced targeted based on interests, age, audiences, CRM data (i.e., your email subscriber database),

lookalikes, and retargeting. This means you can target people who "Like" charities, volunteering, and more.

o Most used ad types by nonprofits:
- *Page Likes* – You can run ads with the goal of getting people to "Like" your Facebook page. This helps to build your overall page Likes but may not yield long-term results due to changing algorithms. Keep in mind, on a low end, only 2% of your page Likes will actually see your messages. However, 2% of 10,000 is more people than 2% of 500.
- *Image Link Ads* – These ads feature one image along with copy above the image and can include a call-to-action button like, "Learn More" below the image that points to a donation page. This is one of the most widely used buttons by nonprofits for its simplicity.
- *Video* – These are very similar to the Image Link Ads but feature a video instead of images. They function the same way in that they include copy above the video and a call-to-action button below the video. These ads are great for fundraising and advocating your organization with a powerful video.
- *Carousel* – These ads can feature up to 10 images or videos within a single ad, each with its own link. This allows you to tell more of a story about your nonprofit, or allow each service to have its own real estate within this ad. These can also be great ads if you have a digital catalog that includes several items, with each image pointing to a specific item in the catalog.

- ▪ *Lead ads* – You can utilize these ads to gain email subscribers. When Facebook users click on the ads, they are pre-populated with the email address they use to log in to Facebook, so it reduces some friction during sign-up. In addition, these ads integrate with Mailchimp, Salesforce Marketing Cloud, and other partners so you can quickly respond to these new email subscribers.
  - ▪ To see all of the ad types available, visit https://www.facebook.com/business/ads-guide.
- Instagram
  - o Because Instagram is owned by Facebook, you can easily advertise on both social media sites within the Facebook Ads platform. The only caution I advise here is that you may not want to advertise on Instagram, based on your fundraising and/or goals and donor demographics. If you're looking at using ads more as advocacy, then Instagram may not be a bad option. However, if you're looking at executing fundraising ads, then you'll need to determine if your demographic is active on Instagram.
  - o Instagram includes similar ad types as Facebook with similar targeting; however, they also offer Story ads. These are video and image ads that appear in a full-screen vertical format between users' stories on Instagram. I'd recommend testing these if your donor base falls in line with the demographics of Instagram's user audience.
- Twitter
  - o Target ads by followers, keywords, email lists (CRM data), and retargeting.

- Twitter currently has 2 different types of ads, which are Follower ads and Promoted Tweets. Follower ads are similar to Facebook's Like ads in that they help you to build more followers for your Twitter profile on a cost-per-follower basis. Promoted tweets allow you to advertise a particular tweet that can point to a donation page or other landing page.
- LinkedIn
  - Target ads by company, job title, email lists (CRM data), education, and interests.
  - Types of ads for LinkedIn include Sponsored Content, Text ads, and InMail ads. Sponsored Content ads appear like updates from your nonprofit in the newsfeed of LinkedIn users, based on whom you target. This means, even if people at certain companies are following your LinkedIn page, you can still reach them with your Sponsored Content ads. They include copy and text, which can point to a donation or landing page. Text ads, which appear only on desktop, include a small thumbnail image, 25-character headline, 75-character description, and link to your donation page.
- Snapchat
  - With Snapchat, you can target your ads based on 300 pre-defined audiences, CRM data, lookalikes, and demographic information.
  - Snapchat has three ad types, which include Snap ads, geo-targeted filters, and lenses. Snap ads are similar to Instagram story ads in that they are video or image ads that appear as full-screen vertical ads between user or content stories. Geo-targeted filters allow Snapchat users to post images or videos with a specific graphic created by your nonprofit within a certain geofence. What this means is that if your

nonprofit is hosting a 5K run, Snapchat users can take pictures or videos and use a graphic that you made exclusively for the event and share it with their friends on Snapchat with the goal of generating awareness (not fundraising). This is great for nonprofits to use if there is an event in which the attendees fill the demographics of Snapchat users because you can geographically target the filter to appear within a parameter around the event. Lenses are the third type of advertising, and also the most expensive. Lenses are the interactive, fun elements that appear on your face in images or videos. These are expensive to create and advertise, so though I mention them, I don't recommend them as a good use of ad budget for your nonprofit at this time. For more information on the latest Snapchat ad products, visit https://forbusiness.snapchat.com/ad-products/.

Why would you use it? Social media ads can be used for many reasons, but I would typically recommend using them as a support to your integrated fundraising campaigns. In addition, the average gift is significantly less than email and SEM. Based on the social media sites reviewed above, the following goals can be met with the corresponding social media channel(s):

- Increase social media audience size: Facebook, Twitter
- Donations: Facebook, Instagram, Twitter, LinkedIn
- List building: Facebook
- Awareness: Facebook, Instagram, Twitter, LinkedIn, Snapchat
- Video Views: Facebook, Instagram, Snapchat

When would you use it? You would use social media ads in conjunction with multi-channel campaigns, whether during the holidays or in conjunction with campaigns throughout the year. In addition, you can get creative and test Lead ads on Facebook at different times of the year. Because the ad products and targeting abilities are so diverse across different social media sites, I believe there is room for nonprofits to really test out different ads throughout the year to determine what works best for their own organizations. What I do recommend against is running ads just for the sake of running ads. I've seen many cases where nonprofits will promote a post on Facebook just because Facebook recommended it. If you do promote posts on Facebook, make sure there is a goal in mind. Don't just promote a post because Facebook says, "People are responding to your post. Would you like to promote it?" This is the easiest way for them to take your money. Have a goal and have a plan for your social media ads.

What kind of results can I expect? The results of your social media ads will depend on your goal. If you're looking to increase Likes or Followers to your Facebook and Twitter pages, then this can be done usually between $0.25-$2.00 per follower. As far as donations are concerned, which is where I recommend you place your focus, expect significantly less gifts and a lower average gift than email and SEM. In addition to gifts, social media ads can also generate awareness for your organization, since other users can like, share, and comment on most ad types on social media.

9

Other Digital Channels to Consider

Content Marketing

Let's talk about content marketing a little bit. A few years ago, after social media started making some noise, the next hot topic was content marketing. In fact, I remember reading an article on *eMarketer* about what areas of digital marketing CMOs were going to invest in during the upcoming year. Content marketing was expected to have the biggest increase in investment, more so than social media.

So, what is content marketing and why should you care? Content marketing is merely asset marketing. The main assets a nonprofit can utilize are images, copy or stories, videos, infographics, e-books, and PDF files like whitepapers or tip sheets. In essence, content marketing is marketing your content. The only problem with that is many nonprofits either don't have much content or haven't organized content in such a way that it's easily available to market.

The great benefit of content marketing is that a great piece of content can be used across multiple digital channels, and sometimes direct mail as well. For example, a powerful video can not only be shared in an email as part of a fundraising campaign, but also the backstory of the video can be told in a blog. The video can appear in social media ads or social media organic posting. Another example of content would be an e-book. For one of my clients, we once put together a disaster response e-book with different tips for times of disaster. This e-book was emailed to existing subscribers as an affirmation email, but it was also used as a downloadable asset in exchange for an email address, which helped acquire new email subscribers. Great images can be used in email, online ads, social media posts, and blogs. My challenge to you is, when defining the types of content your organization will create for the upcoming year, think about how you can use the content to tell your story across multiple channels.

Be intentional about your content plan; don't leave it up to chance. In my opinion, nonprofits should have a person in the organization who is only responsible for procuring, organizing, and distributing content. Perhaps this is a Chief Content Officer or Chief Storytelling Officer. This would be somebody that would work across the organization, being involved with services as well as development. This is somebody that can be on the front lines to get the stories, but also understand why they are getting the stories and how they can be used to increase fundraising opportunities. This is a person that is strategic, analytic, and creative, so it'll be a rare find as many possess two out of these three, but usually not all three.

I've worked for fundraising agencies that have done what are called *resource trips* with nonprofit clients. These trips usually consist of meeting with and interviewing people whom the nonprofit has helped or impacted. Sometimes, this also includes getting pictures of the people and/or some video. With these resource trips, there's usually a creative director in tow to ensure the right questions get asked and the heart of the story comes to life. This is a great way to get content but can fall short in an overarching fundraising strategy because it's executed at a tactical level. In other words, these resources are being gathered with the goal of just fundraising, but lacking insight of the overall fundraising strategic plan.

Fundraising agencies and nonprofits alike should spend more time in the planning process from a content perspective. Most nonprofits are sitting on a stockpile of gems as stories – they just aren't mining them. From a fundraising strategy perspective, plan out a complete year in campaigns and identify the types of stories that will support those campaigns. At a granular level, identify the types of subjects, images, and videos you want to include in your campaigns. Storyboard it out. Heck, maybe your campaigns will all be connected creatively and visually to one theme, rather than 8-12 separate campaigns that have no common thread amongst them.

An ongoing repository for your content can come in the form of a blog. Your blog can either be hosted on your website, a blogging platform like Medium.com, or both. My recommendation is to do both because it helps to expand your reach. Starting out, you can post the exact same content on your company blog as you do on a blogging site. This keeps it simple and easy to manage. By posting on your own site, you are able to capture a warm audience that is likely already familiar with our organization. By posting on a blogging site like Medium, your posts can get discovered and shared organically by an audience that may not be familiar with your nonprofit or its impact. If you do post on a blogging site, make sure you always, always, always, link back to your nonprofit's website. You should wrap up each blog post with, "To learn more about us, please visit www.*yourorganization*.org."

Just thinking of starting a blog can be paralyzing for many nonprofits because resources are already stretched thin between roles. The idea of taking on another project for an individual can be overwhelming. However, blogging is important because it helps improve SEO for your website. It also allows people to see many different dimensions of your organization. If you do start a blog, or already have one up and running, I'd like to offer the following tips and thought-starters that will help set you up for success:

- Start with a vision for your blog. What do you want to accomplish and why? Write it down.
- Identify who your blog audience will be and what you will talk about. Your audience will likely consist of stakeholders, volunteers, donors, and people that need your services. Identify 3-5 audience types and personas. What kind of stories would they want to see and hear?
- Blog ideas: Highlight the services you offer, provide stories of individuals your organization has helped, interview staff and volunteers, and provide a post from the leadership team.
- Create a content calendar. By doing this, it allows you to be organized and designate when particular blog posts will go live. You can schedule blogs that correspond with themes of your fundraising campaigns to help maximize overall impact of your campaigns. By creating a calendar, you also establish deadlines for when you need to have content written, proofed, and ready to publish.
- Make it a team effort. When you spread the contribution of content to the blog throughout the organization, it provides different perspectives, builds internal awareness of the blog, and relieves the pressure from one person doing all the writing.
- Include a CTA on every blog. This may mean ending your blog with a call to volunteer, donate, sign up for email, or contact your organization.
- Format for easy reading. People consume content differently in digital versus direct mail. With digital, it's important to use captivating images, "scannable" content such as bolded words and subheadings, bullet points, and shorter paragraphs.

- Think about what would keep your attention if you were the reader. If your blog post is boring to you, then it's also probably boring to your reader. Make it interesting and have fun with it.

Digital Integration with Direct Mail

We can't talk about digital fundraising without talking about direct mail fundraising. Direct mail still comprises an overwhelming majority of fundraising from individual donors. Even with online giving increasing year over year, some organizations still struggle with how to integrate direct mail with online fundraising. Production schedules of direct mail oftentimes mean that campaigns need to be completely planned and ready to go months before a donor gets a mail piece. The planning and production process for digital starts out several months in advance as well; however, last-minute changes can be implemented the day of a campaign launch.

Because direct mail has been around for so many years, standards have been set, and haven't evolved too much creatively. I've seen many cases where the control direct mail pieces that look dated still beat out newer, flashier, and more graphically advanced direct mail pieces. Yes, it is true...sometimes the control picture of the person with an 80's mullet will drive more revenue than a modern hairstyle. It drives creative people nuts at fundraising agencies because they'd love to evolve the creative, but oftentimes newer doesn't produce results.

This leads to a conundrum when you're seeking to integrate digital with direct mail. Does this mean your emails should look dated and stay away from capabilities in email like motion graphics, iconography, and use of large images? Not exactly. It really provides a testing scenario for your organization when it comes to integrating online and direct mail fundraising appeals. If you have a control mail piece that has proven to be effective in raising money, then you integrate digital elements where you can without everything being "matchy-matchy." This means the offer itself integrates across channels. If the offer is $75 to help fund cancer research in direct mail, then that is also the offer for digital channels. Creatively, you integrate the use of colors, fonts, and logos with that of the control direct mail piece. If the direct mail image seems dated or won't version out correctly in digital because of the dimensions, then test another image.

Another route you can go with a test is to carve out a segment of your direct mail file and associated email addresses. With this segment, you can test completely new creative where the offer, images, iconography, and colors fully match and integrate. The only difference between direct mail and email in this test would be that direct mail would still be in a letter form and include more copy than the email. In this test, you fully integrate the messaging in the campaign, but still cater to how donors interact with the different marketing channels, hence long-form letters for direct mail and short and punchy copy for email.

Integrating direct mail and digital channels has several benefits. Multiple studies have shown that the value of a donor is higher when they give through digital channels. The average gift is higher online than via direct mail, and the frequency of giving is usually higher when donors give in both channels. In addition to fundraising, bridging donors from direct mail to digital can help increase your email and SMS text subscriber base and social media audience size. When direct mail donors make a gift online, it's also a great way to acquire their email addresses. This gives you more ways to reach them and truly start to build out multi-channel success. The following are tips to help integrate your direct mail with digital:

- Include donation page URL within direct mail letter/postcard. The URL should include the same messaging and creative that integrate with the campaign on the direct mail piece.
- Include URL to subscribe for emails. This is great to include in direct mail newsletters but stay away from this tactic with fundraising direct mail pieces. You want those to focus strictly on raising money, not acquiring email subscribers.
- Include text-to-give or SMS sign-up codes. Again, I'd stay away from doing this on fundraising mail pieces and keep it more for direct mail newsletters. However, on the reply device in direct mail fundraising pieces, you could have a checkbox for donors to opt in to receive SMS messages, along with their phone number.
- Tell part of a story in direct mail, then ask a donor to go online to a specific URL to see the rest of the story. This can be done by featuring a video or landing page that shows a compelling story, then you can include an ask for a donation.
- Add an incentive to the donor's gift if they make the gift online. This is a great opportunity for match campaigns, where you can position the offer as "Your gift doubles if you make it online by (specific date)." Get creative in what incentives you offer in direct mail for acquiring online gifts.
- Include callouts for your social media accounts and/or blog. This is another tactic you can easily implement in affirmation direct mail pieces like a newsletter.
- Use postcards as an announcement for an online event like an auction or Giving Tuesday. This is a way to execute a low-cost method of direct mail to fully support an online fundraising campaign. Even if the direct mail piece hits the home just before or after the specific giving date, the postcard will include a URL for the online event or campaign. Just make sure that page stays active and is set up to receive gifts in a large enough window for your direct mail donors to go online and make a gift.

Mobile Fundraising

Mobile fundraising is somewhat of a broad term. It can mean online fundraising through mobile devices, such as donors connecting to your website via mobile internet. It can also mean fundraising through mobile-specific technology like SMS or text-to-give. Though mobile is a small piece of the fundraising pie right now, I expect it to grow significantly in the next 5-10 years. Here are a few stats, provided by MobileCause.com that help affirm this:

- 96% of donors use a smartphone as their primary device
- 98% of text messages sent are read (how's your email open rate looking these days?)
- 51% of web searches happen on mobile devices
- 54% of nonprofit emails are read on mobile devices
- 38% more submissions (gifts, emails, etc.) are made due to mobile-friendly website pages

Though overall donations made from mobile devices have increased, SMS campaigns haven't proven to be a consisten hit just yet. I believe lackluster results from SMS fundraising and messaging by nonprofits come from a lack of nonprofits adapting mobile as a channel. This makes sense because so many nonprofits are still struggling with mastering other digital channels for fundraising. When you add mobile to the mix, this adds yet another channel to manage, which will require more investment and more resources. Most nonprofit clients that I've worked with have expressed interest in bolstering their mobile fundraising programs, but few actually do it because of the hurdle of investment and resources.

Let's take a step back for a moment and talk about ways you can obtain donations through mobile devices. First, there is text-to-give, which is the most common and most popular method. With text-to-give, you text a keyword to a short code. For a made-up example, this would be illustrated by a call to action that says, "Text GIVE to 83733," where GIVE is the keyword and 83733 is the short code.

With text-to-give, donations are a set amount, usually $5 or $10. These donations are billed directly to the donor's phone bill; nonprofits don't have access to the donor's data with these gifts.

Because text-to-give is limited on the size of the gift and organizations don't have access to donor data, another option would be SMS messaging that contains a link to a mobile-optimized donation page. This tactic would be part of a broader SMS strategy that should include both affirmation and fundraising messages, similar to email. Donors and subscribers would still opt into receiving text messages from your organization through the use of texting a keyword to a short code, similar to how they would initialize a text-to-give donation. However, in this case, the nonprofit would own the communication and donation journey with its donors.

I'm a proponent of establishing an overall SMS strategy that coincides with the nonprofit's fundraising or marketing communication calendar. This means you can send SMS messages to promote blog posts, drive users through text messages to URLs that contain videos and stories about your nonprofit, or just a simple motivational message. While I haven't seen enough data to recommend a cadence of text messages or the perfect ratio of affirmation to fundraising messages, I would start at a baseline of no more than two text messages a month and a 3:1 affirmation to fundraising SMS message ratio.

When it comes to fundraising, mobile giving is most effective during events and disaster response. During each of these instances, you have a captive audience, whether in person or via media coverage. Urgency is at a peak because the event will end or need has spiked from a disaster. For events, it's important to spell out exactly what you want donors to do. This means the host or MC needs to literally say, "Take out your phones. Go to your text messages. Text EVENT to 12345." If you only rely on flyers or signage at events to boost mobile fundraising, then you will be leaving money on the table and disappointed with how your mobile fundraising performed.

How do you start a SMS messaging program if you don't have mobile phone numbers from your donors? There are a few ways, and most follow the same tactics you would use to build up your email subscriber list. You can ask for a donor's mobile number at event registrations with an opt-in checkbox for messaging. Including a callout on your website for visitors to subscribe to receive text alerts is another way to organically grow your text subscriber list. A quick way to boost your list size is through mobile appends. These are like email appends in that you partner with a data company to match your donor records with mobile phone number records to create a list of mobile subscribers. If you go that route, you should send an initial text to subscribers to gain permission to add them to mobile messaging. This message could say something like, "As a donor of our organization, we'd like to keep in touch via text message as well. To receive texts, reply to this message with the word YES." This respects the donor's communication and privacy preferences.
The last item I'll touch on for mobile is the importance of using mobile-optimized donation pages for any mobile-based marketing you execute. By now, most organizations have optimized websites for mobile formatting; however, many still have not. From a donor experience perspective, clicking on an ad or SMS message from a mobile device that points to a donation page not formatted for mobile devices is a disaster. The donors have to pinch, squeeze, squint, swipe, and slide just to see the form. Donors won't stick around and will abandon the donation page, possibly never to return again. Once you have donors on your donation page, goal number one is to reduce friction. By having a donation page optimized for mobile, you reduce friction and increase the opportunity to secure the gift.

The channels we've covered so far are the ones most used for fundraising; however, there are many other ways your nonprofit can generate revenue online. New platforms and technology continue to emerge, and time will tell which ones have staying power. The following are four additional fundraising channels that are worth researching to see if they would be a good fit for your organization:

1. **Digital Catalog:** The past few years, I have seen a rise in nonprofits utilizing digital catalogs as a part of the digital fundraising mix. These essentially give the appearance of a normal online shopping experience where donors can "buy" items like nights of shelter, food for a family, Christmas gifts, clothing items, and more. In reality, donors are not really buying anything, but rather making a donation that is equivalent to the item represented in the picture and description. As a tip, if you are a nonprofit that uses this tactic, it's important that you include a disclaimer stating that it is a catalog of equivalencies, and the items represent the needs of the organization.

    Digital catalogs can be an effective way to engage the donor because they show different needs and provide somewhat of an instant gratification to the donor by showing how their donation will be used. Psychologically, wouldn't you rather know your $50 is going to provide a coat for a young child rather than $50 just going to the organization? I would, and so would most people. This is why catalogs can be effective.

    The downside of catalogs is that they can be costly to build. Even if you use a platform like Shopify.com for your catalog, you still may want some customization done that requires a website developer. It also takes time to plan out what items will be included in the catalog, along with the titles and descriptions of each item. Digital catalogs can be dynamic and have many uses, whether it's for the holidays, disaster response, or to support campaigns at other times of the year. It also presents new ways to engage with your donors and learn what types of offers best resonate with them by offering different items.

2. **Peer to Peer:** This fundraising style relies heavily on a nonprofit's biggest advocates and word-of-mouth marketing. Campaigns are usually structured with an overall revenue goal, theme, and cause. Individuals can set up their own fundraising pages and invite others to contribute towards the fundraiser by a specific date. These individual campaign pages are even more effective if the person tells his or her story about their experience with the organization or the cause it is supporting. For example, if a person is trying to raise money for a 5K run that benefits cancer research, then that individual's campaign page may talk about his or her story of overcoming cancer or a loved one that battled cancer.

It's called Peer to Peer because it relies on fundraising from individuals in their circle of influence. It's kind of like the Avon of fundraising because you're tapping into your friends and family to buy in to your campaign. Except, instead of beauty products, people can make a donation to support a higher cause that positively impacts others.

Managing a peer-to-peer program is less about managing donors, and more about managing your top individual fundraising advocates that are connected to your organization. They should be treated like major donors because their influence can generate a lot of revenue for your organization. According to research, the top 10% of your peer-to-peer fundraisers will generate more than half of the campaign revenue. Get to know these 10%, so that they can help you out year after year. According to Fundly, 55-64 is the average age of the most active peer-to-peer fundraising demographic.

3. **Voice:** We've now arrived at a time in history where you can literally donate money to a nonprofit by the sound of your voice. This is the biggest game changer in digital fundraising since digital became a channel. Starting with Amazon's Alexa, all you have to do is say, "Make a donation to (insert nonprofit name here)," to which Alexa replies, "How much would you like to donate?" That's it – gift accepted with minimal effort and no friction. Your donors' gifts are secured by using the payment information that exists in their Amazon accounts. An appealing part about this service is that you have access to the donor's gift amount, email address, and physical address. As a nonprofit, you do have to register for this service. To learn more, visit https://pay.amazon.com/us/charity.

My hope is that other voice-activated platforms make this feature available as well. I imagine that CTAs for digital fundraising campaigns will begin to evolve. Instead of just including a donate now button on websites, emails, and donation pages, I believe we'll start to see more CTAs like, "Say, Alexa, make a donation to...." The time saved and ease of use alone make voice donations a channel poised to explode in growth.

4. **AmazonSmile:** While we're on the topic of Amazon, they also offer another service for nonprofits called AmazonSmile. This service allows users to shop on Amazon just as they normally would; however, Amazon will donate 0.5% of your purchase on eligible products to the charitable organization of your

choice. While 0.5% doesn't sound like much, it can add up over time. Besides, this is easy money that you don't have to ask people to donate because it's done automatically with each purchase. Simply register your nonprofit with AmazonSmile, then communicate to your donors via direct mail and digital how they can help further support your organization through purchases they already make through Amazon. Learn more at https://org.amazon.com.

At this point of the book, you've got enough knowledge, tips, and tricks to start making incremental differences with your nonprofit's digital fundraising. Even if your role isn't directly involved in digital fundraising, you should now have enough information to provide a picture of digital fundraising and be able to better follow conversations about digital. It might even give you the ammo to ask the right questions of your digital team, agency, and partners.

For the next section of the book, we'll move into how to organize and plan your digital fundraising efforts. You can have all the digital fundraising channel knowledge in the world, but if you don't know how to strategically make it come together, then you'll be wasting a lot of dollars that your donors trusted you to put to good use. I look at it as if the digital channels were instruments of a talented orchestra, and strategy the conductor. Sure, the orchestra could do a jam session, and it *could be* a beautiful, organized chaos, but a conductor creates a live masterpiece and ensures the direction of the instruments is perfect. The result is always a standing ovation. That said, let's talk about how to put your digital fundraising orchestra into masterful use – only, instead, your standing ovation will come in the form of monetary donations.

Section 2: Digital Campaign Planning & Campaign Overview

10

VOSTEK™ Introduction

Throughout my professional career, especially in marketing and fundraising roles, I began to notice a pattern with a majority of my clients. They were passionate about their product, service, or cause and eager to let the world know all about it. This eagerness oftentimes led to falling into the "dog-squirrel syndrome." You know how dogs walk along a path, then they see a squirrel, get completely distracted, and start running off the course of the path to catch the squirrel? Yeah, it happens to humans and companies too. Many times, organizations have a goal, and maybe even a strategy. But then the squirrel shows its face in the form of a new social media site, best-practices article, or other factor. Organizations abandon strategy and chase after that squirrel, losing site of the plan they had in place.

What I've found is that many organizations don't have a proper framework for their strategy; therefore, it's easy to get distracted and swerve off course. There are minimal levers of accountability to identify if and when this distraction occurs. As a result, I've created a strategy model called VOSTEK™, which stands for Vision, Objective, Strategy, Tactics, Execution, and KPIs. In essence, this model *is* the blueprint of digital fundraising, or any fundraising for that matter. Every action, from planning to execution, can be contained within this model.

What's important to note about VOSTEK™ is that each step is done in order. First, you create your vision, then objectives, then strategy, and so on. I have witnessed marketing and fundraising plans fail because either there is no vision, objectives are too vague, or organizations put tactics before strategy. The VOSTEK™ framework helps you keep an eye on all of the important planning factors that impact your outcome.

I've utilized VOSTEK™ with many of my clients over the years, including nonprofits and Fortune 100 companies. From small community-based organizations to $1 billion+ companies, this model has proven an effective framework for strategy planning. Beyond business planning, I also use VOSTEK™ as a way to capture my personal goals and life planning. It's a great model to identify where you are, where you're failing, and where you need to course-correct. Let's jump into each component.

Vision

"It all starts with a vision." I have this written on a whiteboard in my home office. If I need to erase this phrase to make space for other ideas and drawings, I always go back and rewrite it on the board when I'm done. It's a reminder that everything you do links up to a higher cause. When it comes to fundraising, it's easy to get caught up in a sales mode and the execution of marketing tactics to transact donations. Individuals and organizations can lose sight of *why* they're raising the money in the first place. Sure, they'll remember that they're raising money to help others, but it's deeper than that. The money that is raised helps to literally provide peace, comfort, hope, health, preservation, and security to humans, animals, and the environment. It's an amazing thing!

Your organization should have a vision. Your fundraising campaigns should have a vision. This vision sets the tone from the top down that everything you do will be done with the intent of accomplishing this vision. I sometimes ask my nonprofit clients, "What does your nonprofit want to be when it grows up?" It doesn't matter if your nonprofit is a start-up or has been around for decades, the question is still relevant. For new nonprofits, it can help to define and shape how it markets and fundraises. For mature nonprofits, this question can prompt discussions to identify if gaps exist in how it operates versus what its stated mission says. A nonprofit's vision says *why* they are in business and comes typically in the form of a mission or vision statement.

Taking this concept a little deeper, what is the vision for your digital fundraising? I think of this as your view from the winner's podium. Let's assume you've accomplished all that you possibly can through your digital fundraising efforts. What does that look like? When creating your digital fundraising vision, this is where you think big and bold. It's a blue-sky approach that defines the perfect world view of your accomplishment with as much detail as possible. Your vision shouldn't be about money, but rather about impact. It's not about how many dollars you raised, but how those dollars made a difference and defining that difference. Your vision documents a target to achieve.

If you don't feel inspired when you say or read your vision, then I'd challenge you to rewrite it. After all, it takes bold leadership to create a bold vision, but it also takes the tenacity of this leadership to diffuse this vision through the organization and obtain buy-in. If leadership isn't inspired by the vision, then how can they expect others to rally behind it? This is why it's so important that leadership, whether at an organizational or development level in nonprofits, agrees upon and supports the vision. From a development perspective, a bold vision for fundraising inspires other team members to give their best and produce their best work in order to accomplish the vision. However, if the fundraising vision is bold, but the development leader doesn't seem to have bought into the vision, then his or her team members will see it and success will be limited. So here's my advice: Create a bold vision that you believe in, share this vision, get buy-in from others, and keep this vision top of mind by printing or writing it out where you can see it every day.

As we go through the VOSTEK™ framework, we'll use the following digital fundraising vision as an example: "*We will make the world a better place by eradicating hunger and providing food and hope to men, women, and children through digital technology that warms donors' hearts and unlocks generosity in abundance.*"

Objectives

Once your vision is established, you create objectives (or goals) that will help your organization accomplish your digital fundraising vision. These objectives define the results and outcomes and are usually completed on at least an annual basis, though you may also have three- or five-year objectives. When you're creating digital fundraising objectives, it's a good idea to limit them to no more than 3-5 objectives. By limiting objectives to a smaller number, it helps your organization to remain focused on accomplishing these objectives. When you have too many objectives to accomplish, it can be difficult to manage or allocate the necessary resources to achieve all of the objectives.

This is the part of the VOSTEK™ framework where you can utilize SMART goals. In this case, SMART stands for:

- **Specific** – The more specific the better. It's hard to hit a moving or vague target, so be precise with the goal you are attempting to accomplish.
- **Measurable** – A professor of mine in grad school would say, "What gets measured gets done." Is your goal measurable? Measuring usually requires numbers, so what numbers are you communicating in your objectives?

- **Attainable** – Do you have the resources, staff, technology, etc. to attain the objective you create?
- **Realistic** – In addition to a goal being attainable, is it realistic that you can actually complete it? Some may say that it is redundant for an objective to be attainable and realistic. After all, aren't those the same thing? Not quite – let me explain. From a nonprofit perspective, it's completely attainable to execute a digital campaign in-house that requires email, social media, and paid search. Let's assume you have the staff and skill set to do this. Totally attainable. However, if the workload of this digital campaign is going to require overtime of evenings and weekends for weeks on end, or lacks the budget, then it's not quite realistic. Attainable, yes…realistic, maybe not. Your SMART goal should be one that is both; otherwise it may not be achieved.
- **Time-bound** – A goal without time parameters is just a "nice idea." By putting a deadline on your objective, you create a target that has an expiration date. This creates urgency and an importance in accomplishing the objective.

Here's an example of a SMART goal: *"Increase online fundraising revenue by 10% during the next fiscal year."*

In this example, it's specific (increase online revenue), measurable (by 10%), attainable, realistic, and time-bound (during the next fiscal year). As it pertains to VOSTEK™, if you achieve your objectives, then you should also achieve your vision.

Strategy

After defining your objectives, you then develop your strategy. Your strategy defines *how* you accomplish your objectives. Strategy, by nature, is a long-term plan that sets the foundation for tactics. It typically isn't highly detailed, leaving wiggle room for your tactics to do the heavy lifting. Your digital strategy may identify resources, focus on channels, or even touch on how you will impact donor life cycles or giving levels.

An example of a strategy statement may be to *"Utilize multiple digital channels to attract and acquire new donors."* This statement displays **how** you will support the objective we used above, *"Increase online fundraising revenue by 10% during the next fiscal year."*

Though a strategy statement may sound basic because it is oftentimes distilled down to one sentence, there is a lot of critical thought, research, and discovery that must occur before a strategy is created. For example, if you have no experience or knowledge about digital fundraising at all, then creating a digital fundraising strategy may be a challenge. You have to understand the lay of the land. This means understanding what technologies are available to validate if your strategy will even have a shot at success. It also means having at least a high-level knowledge of the different digital marketing channels, how they are used, and what data is available from each channel. Of course, having the "battle-tested" experience of previously running digital fundraising campaigns will help sharpen your strategy as well. To sum it up, I've discovered the following eight inputs that get baked into a great strategy:

- **Analytics** – This may include previous campaign, gift, and donor data, specifically email metrics, Google Analytics, gift frequency, and more.
- **Technology** – Understanding of internal marketing technology, external marketing technology that exists, and emerging marketing technology.
- **Budgets** – Indeed, your budget can limit your strategy, so having a grasp on your budget does matter.
- **Creative** – Understanding your organization's or agency's abilities with creative content as well as the results of any creative tests conducted in digital or direct mail.

- **Goals (Organization, Department)** – Ensuring that your strategy lines up with your organization's goals is extremely important, which is why *strategy* follows *vision* in VOSTEK™.
- **Capabilities** – Understanding the digital fundraising and creative capabilities of your staff and agency.
- **Industry Trends** – Studying industry reports and case studies for digital fundraising will help to inform your strategy and also help you validate strategic decisions to other stakeholders.
- **Stakeholder Meetings** – Understanding the politics and agendas of other stakeholders within and external to your organization may help to adjust your digital fundraising strategy.

Mistakes will be made along the way, but so will successes. Each of these helps inform your strategy as it grows more sound. In digital fundraising, technologies and best practices evolve quickly. This has more of an impact on tactics rather than strategy; however, you may have to modify strategies based on the speed of change.

Tactics
After defining your strategy, you're ready to map out the tactics. While strategy encompasses your long-term planning, tactics are the shorter-term, adjustable methods that accomplish the strategy. Using the example strategy statement of *"Utilize multiple digital channels to attract and acquire new donors,"* you then have to identify what tools and methods you will use to accomplish the strategy. In this case, your tactics may be email, social media community management, website content, and digital ads. Each of these tactics helps support your strategy.

Typically, each tactic your organization incorporates also comes with a price tag. When nonprofits started to make the digital transformation a part of fundraising strategy, it required investment in a website. Web content became a tactic, but soon email followed. This required investment in website content and email platforms and content. Then came search engine marketing, which resulted in investment in website content, email platforms and content, and SEM ad buys. Next came online display ads, social media, and mobile. You can see how this can grow and expand quickly, depleting budgets and resources. However, many of these digital costs are now simply the cost of doing business in fundraising. Nonprofits are slowly shifting money from direct mail and out-of-home fundraising budgets to build out digital competencies. The costs of fundraising don't proportionately coincide with increases in fundraising budgets, as nonprofits are faced implementing more tactics and channels with the same or slightly higher budgets.

Let me provide an example of why tactics must follow strategy, not the other way around. Imagine you decide to embark on a 15-day European vacation with your spouse or significant other. Imagine your trip started like this: You drive to your local airport, buy two tickets to a country with the soonest departure, get on a plane, land somewhere in Europe, get off the plane, then figure out what hotel in which you will be staying. Sounds adventurous, right? I'm sure some people would appreciate that.

There are several problems with this approach though. These would include not packing a suitcase of clothing and items you will need for your vacation, paying more for a ticket because you bought it at the last minute, and spending way more time getting lost because you didn't know where you were going and didn't bother to research the area. Going to Europe seemed like a cool idea because you've heard great things about it; however, the implementation of vacation tactics was a disaster because you didn't have an overall vacation plan. This cost you time, money, discomfort, and maybe your relationship. Oddly, these are the same things nonprofits sacrifice (along with impact) when they prioritize tactics over strategy.

I continually see nonprofits executing at a tactical level, but they have no digital strategy in mind. They think, "Hey, let's do social media!" Then, the next step they take is putting together a social media messaging calendar, oftentimes not tied to any business goals. This same scenario plays out with email, content, pay-per-click ads, and so on. It's the ol' approach of "I've heard this is hot, so let's do something like that. Now."

By now, you should understand that once your strategy is established, the tactics will enable your strategy. Here are a few examples of tactics and questions you should ask as you build them out:

- **Digital content creation** – What type of content will resonate most with your existing and potential donors?
- **Email communication** – What messaging themes, tone, and frequency will you use?
- **List building (audience building)** – How will you build your email subscriber list and social media audience size?
- **Search engine marketing** – What campaigns, themes, and ad copy will you create in order to acquire donors, email subscribers, or volunteers?
- **Social media community management** – How frequently will you post organic content, and what will you say?

Execution
Upon completion of mapping out the tactics that will fulfill your strategy, it's time to understand and/or document how you will execute these tactics. Execution is where the rubber meets the road, and leads the way to actions that support the tactics. This part of VOSTEK™ contains the most granular pieces that consume the most time resources. From an organizational level, a fundraising strategist may be involved in developing the vision, objectives, strategy, and tactics. The people involved with execution are the specialists that

144

are designing emails, copywriting, setting up and monitoring campaigns in Google and Facebook, and so on.

There can be many ways to execute a single tactic from a creative and technical perspective. Creatively, an organic social media post is a tactic that can be executed either through an image, video, or standalone copy. Technically, a Facebook post can be executed either through Facebook directly, or a third-party platform like Hootsuite. A creative execution with email may include testing different images, fonts, or layouts. Technically, an email can be executed through a number of different platforms, including Mailchimp, Blackbaud, Constant Contact, or others. Therefore, execution can shift between variables without impacting strategy.

As you identify the tactics, you will also identify how you will execute these tactics. In the section above, we identified tactics and questions to ask as you build out the tactics. Revisiting that section, let's now map tactics with execution as follows:

- Tactic: *Digital content creation*
    - Execution: blogs (and blog platforms), videos, whitepapers, slideshows, memes, infographics, etc.
- Tactic: *Email communication*
    - Execution: image heavy vs. text heavy, messaging, cadence, theme, email service provider (ESPs)
- Tactic: *List building (audience building)*
    - Execution: email list building, freemium creation, Facebook Likes, Twitter followers, etc.
- Tactic: *Search engine marketing*
    - Execution: platforms (Google/Bing/Google Ads Grant), ad copy, landing page content, keywords, themes, etc.
- Tactic: *Social media community management*
    - Execution: platforms (Facebook, Twitter, Instagram, etc.), types of content, editorial calendars,

copywriting, comment monitoring and responding, etc.

KPIs

Your strategy means nothing unless it can be measured. Otherwise, how will you know if you've been successful? Measurements quantify strategy and help you make important decisions that can impact creative, marketing channel and technology investment, time and delivery of emails, and more. Tracking various metrics helps you identify what marketing and messaging works, what doesn't work, and what needs to be modified or tested.

When it comes to digital fundraising, it's easy to get lost in the metrics and drown in a flood of data. To illustrate this, look at a sample of the following metrics by fundraising channel:

- **Website**
    - Number of sessions
    - Average time on site
    - Bounce rate
    - Page Views
    - Number of conversions
    - Conversion rate
    - Percentage of mobile visitors (along with desktop and tablet visitors)
- **Email**
    - Number of opens
    - Open rate
    - Number of clicks
    - Click-through rate
    - Number of unsubscribes
    - Unsubscribe rate
    - Number reported as SPAM
    - SPAM rate
    - Revenue per thousand emails

- **Online Display Ads**
  - Number of impressions
  - Number of clicks
  - Click-through rate
  - Total cost
  - Cost per click
  - View-through rate
  - Number of conversions
  - Cost per conversion
- **Search Engine Marketing**
  - Number of impressions
  - Number of clicks
  - Click-through rate
  - Total cost
  - Costs per click
  - Number of conversions
  - Cost per conversion
- **Social Media Ads**
  - Number of impressions
  - Number of clicks
  - Click-through rate
  - Total cost
  - Costs per click
  - Number of conversions
  - Cost per conversion
- **Social Media Posts**
  - Number of Likes
  - Number of Followers
  - Number of engagements
  - Engagement rate
  - Number of comments
- **Mobile SMS**
  - Number of opens
  - Open rate

- Number of clicks
- Click-through rate
- Number of conversions
- Conversion rate

These are 49 different metrics between 7 marketing channels. Though these 49 may be deemed the most important metrics by each channel, these are not all the available metrics for each channel. For website metrics alone, you can probably mine 100+ data points. Add into the mix any split or segmentation testing, and you have even more metrics to wrangle in. If you're not into data, then you probably have already skipped to the next paragraph, or are nodding off. If data is "your thing," then you feel like you've just uncovered King Solomon's mine and are ready to go digging for more data and metrics.

No matter which side of the fence you're on when it comes to data infatuation, this one thing remains true: You can't be successful if 49 metrics are your most important metrics. It's too much to keep your eye on. That's not to say that these 49 metrics are not important or should be ignored. It just means that you would have 49 boxes to check every single day, especially when in fundraising campaign mode. In addition, we've only looked at digital marketing channel metrics, and haven't included other marketing channel or marketing program metrics. Feeling anxious yet?

Though many metrics exist, it is your sole purpose in fundraising life to pare those down to the absolute, most important metrics that measure overall digital fundraising success. These are your *key performance indicators*, or KPIs. If you were able to quantify your *vision*, the KPIs would tell you how *hot* or *cold* your organization is in accomplishing that vision. Do not establish a KPI that you are unable to measure, such as a feeling or emotion. In the same vein, don't institute a KPI because it sounds good, but don't have a mechanism to measure it. For example, if you can't effectively measure the lifetime value of a donor, then that shouldn't be a KPI. A good idea to is to create a dashboard-style document that fits the KPIs on one sheet and can be shared with the nonprofit's leadership team. You'll have to identify which are most important to you, but here are some examples of KPIs you might consider using:

- Cost to acquire a new donor
- Average revenue per donation
- Return on Investment (ROI)
- *Alternative KPI:* Equate dollars to impact for a quarter or year (e.g., provided 125,333 meals)

The Digital Fundraising Funnel

Up to this point, we've gone over the Digital Fundraising Ecosystem and explored each digital channel. In addition, we've walked through VOSTEK™, which helps to put structure around your strategy and planning efforts. Now, let's talk about the Digital Fundraising Funnel, which overlays strategy, tactics, and measurement along the donor journey. If you've been involved in sales, marketing, or business development, you've likely seen a similar funnel.

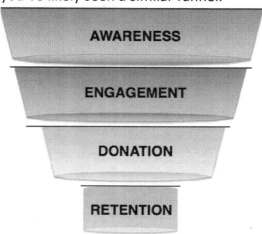

Each level of the funnel is accompanied by several tactics that can be measured. Let's define each level and review those tactics and measurements as follows:

- **Awareness** – This ties into brand or campaign recognition. How do people find out about you? If you're a smaller or newer organization, Awareness is the act of making your community or donors aware of who you are or what you do. If you're a larger or more mature organization, Awareness is all about staying relevant and reminding people that you exist.
  - ○ *Digital tactics and measurements:*

AWARENESS	
Tactic	Measurement
SEO	Number of Website Visitors
Google Grants	Impressions
Online Display Ads	Impressions
Social Media Community Management	Reach or Impressions
Promoted Accounts	Page Likes of Followers
List Building	Email List Size or Mobile Opt-Ins
SEM Ads	Impressions

- **Engagement** – Once people are aware of your brand or campaign, how will you engage with them? This audience of people is usually one that has opted to receive communication from you by following your social media accounts, signing up for your email list, or opting in to receive SMS messages from your organization. Engagement is about keeping their attention once you have it and will require a solid communication plan with a consistent frequency.
  - ○ *Digital tactics and measurements:*

ENGAGEMENT

Tactic	Measurement
Email	Email Opens and Clicks
Website	Time on Site
Google Ads	Clicks
E-Newsletter	Email Opens and Clicks
Social Media Community Management	Number of Comments, Likes, or Shares of Content

- **Donation** – This is the point of the funnel where the donor completes a financial transaction with your nonprofit. Many tactics can be used to push traffic to an online donation page, where the donor can make a gift. A key for your organization is to ensure the easiest, quickest experience for your donor to make that online gift while you have his or her attention.
  - *Digital tactics and measurements:*

DONATION	
Tactic	Measurement
Google Ads	Donation Amount, Average Donor Value, Donation per Channel, Conversion Rate, ROI
Donation Page	
Text-to-Give	
Website Banners & Lightboxes	
Online Catalog	
Social Media Ads	
Email	

- **Retention** – For many sales and marketing funnels, you will see it end at the point of donation or purchase; however, this leaves an important level out of the funnel. Once you obtain a new donor or gift from an existing donor, it's extremely important to retain that donor. As you've probably found out from your own experience, it's much less expensive to obtain gifts from existing donors than it is to acquire new donors. That said, once you obtain that gift, nurture those donors. Make them feel appreciated and communicate with them regularly so they recognize their importance.

o   *Digital tactics and measurements:*

RETENTION	
Tactic	Measurement
Sustainer Program	Donor Lifetime Value,
Loyalty Program	Frequency of Donation
E-Newsletters & Email	Email Unsubscribes
Surveys & Quizzes	Survey & Quiz Responses
SMS Messaging	Mobile Opt-Outs

The goal for any fundraiser should be to make it through the funnel from Awareness to Retention for individual donors. This means that you would have successfully transformed somebody from not knowing who you are into becoming a devoted and giving advocate to your nonprofit. In order to maximize organizational success, each level requires your perpetual planning and attention. For example, when you stop focusing on Awareness or Engagement, then you limit the pool of potential donors. This erodes brand affinity and hurts multi-year donor value because you end up with a smaller cohort of new donors for that particular year. Adversely, when you don't focus on Retention, then you have a higher rate of donor attrition, which also negatively impacts your revenue. There's only so much budgeted money to go around, so you'll need to evaluate the correct amounts for your organization to invest in each level of the funnel.

11

Digital Fundraising Planning & Prioritizing

Annual Digital Fundraising Planning

Fundraising is a cycle that normally repeats every calendar year. Certainly, the fourth quarter of the calendar year is a given when it comes to having a fundraising plan in place. Outside of the fourth quarter, you may have annual events or campaigns that you run throughout the year that provide some regularity and expected communication from your donors. If your organization is involved in disaster response, then this can impact timing of planned campaigns. Despite this anomaly, your organization should be planning at least 12 months at a time when it comes to digital and overall fundraising.

The following is an 11-step approach you can take when it comes to your annual planning:
1) Run through VOSTEK™ exercise for the year
   a. Plan a 1- to 2-day meeting with your immediate team (or leadership team) and start going through each component of VOSTEK™
   b. To keep this from being a boring and drab meeting, try to hold it off-site and provide food/catering
2) Identify the 3-4 most important objectives
   a. As you brainstorm and come up with several objectives that you want to accomplish in the upcoming year, narrow the list down to the 3-4 most important to your mission

b. These 3-4 objectives should be clear to your team, and I'd recommend even printing out and posting them somewhere that you will frequently look

3) Identify fundraising/marketing programs (3-4)
   a. With your objectives in place, you now have some direction on what kinds of marketing programs you'd like to execute for the year
   b. Many times, marketing programs are linked to services within the nonprofit
   c. For example, your nonprofit may offer feeding, housing, and rehab services; therefore, your marketing programs may line up to each of these internal services

4) Identify budget for the year
   a. With your marketing programs identified, you can now start to estimate budgets for your marketing programs
   b. If possible, run through budget scenarios where you look at your previous year's fundraising budget and revenue outcome along with how that would look if you invested $X more or $X less
   c. Present your budget and objectives to your finance board (or person who holds the purse strings) for approval
   d. Sometimes, this budget is given to you before you even start the VOSTEK™ exercise, but it's still good to run through the scenarios in case you need to request more fundraising investment

5) Identify fundraising/marketing campaigns (8-13)
   a. Now that your budget and marketing programs are settled, review the previous year's digital fundraising campaigns to identify the successes and opportunities
   b. Next, brainstorm a list of new ideas that may be viable fundraising campaigns over the next year
   c. Between your proven campaigns and ideas for new campaigns, whittle that list down to 8-13 different campaigns

you can execute over a 12-month period that line up to your marketing programs and goals

    d. As a rule of thumb, campaigns should normally run between 4-6 weeks

6) Calendar out flight dates for campaigns

    a. With your campaigns completed, break out your calendar and take a look at the upcoming year

    b. Write your campaign flight dates on a calendar and create an Excel, Word, or Google Docs file for the dates that can be easily communicated with others

7) Identify technology to execute plan

    a. Take inventory of existing technology that has helped with marketing efforts

    b. Identify strengths and weaknesses of existing marketing technology

    c. If needed, research other technology solutions to power the next year's marketing plan

    d. Prepare to build a business case for your organization's finance board if additional marketing technology investment will be required

8) Identify staffing to execute plan

    a. Identify existing digital fundraising skill sets available within your organization

    b. For skill sets needed to execute marketing plan, determine if you need to train existing staff, hire a freelancer for projects, or hire additional full-time staff

    c. Prepare to build a business case for your organization's finance board if additional human capital is required to execute fundraising plan

9) Meet with stakeholders to review plan

    a. After your fundraising plan is finalized, it's time to get it blessed by others in the organization

b. Meet with your organization's leadership team to communicate your digital fundraising goals, programs, campaigns, and dates

c. Gather any input from these stakeholders that may result in modifications to your plan

10) Schedule annual plan meeting to review high-level plan

a. If there are changes to your plan after the stakeholder meeting, revise your plan and present this plan again

b. If there are no changes to your plan, then prepare to review this high-level plan with other departments in your organization to make them aware of the digital fundraising efforts in the upcoming year

11) Kick off meeting with digital team to launch work

a. Once the fundraising plan has been communicated with your organization's senior leadership and department heads, it's time to formally kick off the work with your digital team

b. This kick-off meeting should include any team members that will touch the digital fundraising efforts, including website developers, email specialists, graphic designers, copywriters, digital (and direct mail) strategists, digital media managers, social media specialists, and project managers

c. The goal of this meeting is to essentially align the troops and communicate the campaigns for the upcoming year and solicit feedback to identify gaps or opportunities to improve the plan and develop creative briefs for each campaign

d. After this meeting, there are a few different paths you can take, depending on what works best for your organization:

i) *Annual campaign planning meeting* – This would encompass 1-2 days of meetings to review all creative briefs and discuss strategy and execution of all digital fundraising campaigns for the year

ii) *Semi-annual campaign planning meeting* – This meeting may last a day and includes the review of all creative briefs and a discussion of strategy and execution of all digital fundraising campaigns for the next 6 months

iii) *Quarterly campaign planning meeting* – Quarterly campaign meetings may last half a day and include the review of all creative briefs and a discussion of strategy and execution of all digital fundraising campaigns for the next quarter

Types of Annual Planning Assets

It wouldn't be wise to hop in a boat and sail across the ocean without a map, compass, or plan. Nor would it be wise to execute digital fundraising without a plan or compass that provides direction for each campaign. There are a few important assets you'll want to create to better organize your annual digital fundraising plan and individual campaigns for the year. While you may have your own secret sauce of documentation to help keep your efforts on track, I recommend the following four assets to help with planning:

- **Annual Campaign Calendar** – When I mentioned calendaring out flight dates for campaigns in the section above, this is the asset you would utilize. You would create a view of your 12-month fundraising year that includes launch and end dates (flight dates) of campaigns. Ideally, this calendar would contain all marketing touchpoints, including digital, direct mail, out-of-home, and any other marketing channels. An easy way to line this up in a grid is to have the columns represent months or weeks of the year, and rows for each marketing channel.
- **Marketing Channel Master Calendar** – This view of your marketing is specific to a marketing sub-channel. In this case, Digital is the channel, and the sub-channels can be Email, Blog, Social Media, Google Ads, Bing Ads, Online Display Ads, etc. The set-up of this document can easily follow the format of the Annual Campaign Calendar. In fact, if you're using Excel, this could actually be a separate tab within the same

file. Each tab can be the channel name, such as Digital, Direct Mail, Out-of-Home, etc. The columns would list out the months or weeks of the year, and the rows along the side would include each sub-channel. For Digital, this would provide a complete view of all your digital activities throughout the year by each sub-channel.

- **Digital Media Calendar** – If you're doing any kind of digital media buys like Google Ad Grants, Google Ads, Bing Ads, or Facebook Ads, you'll want to create a system to track your planned and actual media spend. What I've found to be helpful is setting up a spreadsheet that includes the digital marketing channel, the type of ad, flight dates, planned budget, actual spend, and utilization of the budget (actual spend divided by planned budget). The set-up would look similar to this example for each digital media channel:

	September 9/4-9/28 Ad Type: Video Ad		
	Target Audience: (description of audience goes here)		
	FB		
	Planned	Actual	Utilization
Campaign 1	$ 3,569	$ 1,666	47%

- **Creative/Campaign Briefs** – A creative brief (sometimes called a campaign brief) is essentially a strategic document that communicates the goals of the campaign and guides the direction of creative, technical, and marketing execution. I've worked at a few different marketing agencies, and when it comes to creative briefs, there are 2 things in common between agencies. First, the creative brief is the most important asset for guiding the direction of your campaign. Second, creative briefs are different at every agency. I've even Googled "creative brief examples" in order to get an idea of what other people include in creative briefs. There's

158

no standard; however, there are some items that are included in almost every creative brief. As you're putting together a creative brief for your campaigns, consider using the following as guidance:

- o Campaign name
- o Date of the brief
- o Author of the brief
- o If modified, date of modification
- o If modified, author of modification
- o Goal(s) of campaign
- o Description of campaign
- o Description of tests within campaign (if applicable)
- o Campaign offer (if applicable)
- o Target audience
- o Messaging and theme of campaign
- o Creative considerations for campaign (colors, tone, logos, image/video description, taglines, subject lines, etc.)
- o List and description of marketing channels and how they will be used
- o Deliverables (list of marketing assets)
- o Deployment schedule of each marketing asset
- o Risks (if applicable)
- o Team member roles and responsibilities
- o Additional section for notes
- o Reference items
  - ▪ Screenshots of previous creative, if applicable
  - ▪ Test results, if campaign previously tested any factors
  - ▪ Campaign performance results, if this campaign was previously active

The four assets we just outlined have saved me a lot of time when it comes to planning, tracking, and communicating fundraising plans.

Some of the assets I built from scratch, based upon needs I identified with clients or agencies. I'd challenge you to do the same where you see gaps in processes or communication with your own nonprofits. Opportunities to improve the organization of your marketing often come out of frustration with communicating or finding information. In my case, I was constantly looking in Google Ads, emails, and multiple files to track digital media spending for campaigns. It was crazy. I had to take the time to determine the kind of view of the data I would need, then built out a template for tracking digital media budget and ad spend. This not only helped me but other team members as well to stay on track and organized. Are there planning assets you can create that can ease frustration with your team?

How to Prioritize Your Digital Fundraising Channels

"If you had $10,000 to invest in your digital fundraising efforts, how would you invest it?" This is a question I get a few times a year from different nonprofit clients. There's no one-size-fits-all answer because it depends on overall fundraising strategy, technology, fundraising maturity, personnel, and other factors. From a foundational standpoint, the way to prioritize your digital marketing channels is by the quickest path to the donation. This path will look different when comparing a startup community nonprofit versus an established international organization, but there are some sound approaches to prioritizing channels across any organization. The following order is one approach:

1. **Your Website:** This is your organization's online home, where people will go to learn more about your cause. Just like your real house that you go home to at night, make sure it's clean, in order, and ready for company. You want your guests to have a good experience. Make it easy for people to make donations or sign up for email updates from your homepage. According to an M+R study, around 1% of website visitors will make a donation and sign up for your emails.

2. **Email:** Once your website is in order and set up for donations, focus on building your email list and developing your email communication plan. Your email template should have a "Donate Now" button on each email to allow donors to easily make a gift. Your emails will contain a mix of fundraising messages and affirmation/engagement messages. Because you can incorporate video on landing pages, images, and design, this is one of the best ways to engage with your existing donors and subscribers to tell the story of your organization. It's also one of the best digital fundraising channels.

3. **Search Engine Marketing:** SEM is the next building block in digital fundraising after you've established email. You can register for Google for Nonprofits and get up to $10,000 a month in free search ads on Google. If you don't qualify, it's still a good idea to jump into SEM, especially around the holidays, because of the direct response nature of this channel. One of the keys for SEM is to have a well-designed, mobile-optimized landing page to which the ads can point.

4. **Social Media:** Although this comes in at No. 4, you should definitely establish your social media accounts and do some posting after your website is complete. But when you look at social media as a fundraising channel, it falls after SEM. That's because social media is, well, social. It's not the best place to expect a gold mine of donations. However, you'll certainly get some gifts through social media ads. Over the past year, I've witnessed the importance of social media as an influence channel, as opposed to a direct fundraising channel. For example, the ability now exists where, if a person makes a gift in another online channel or direct mail, you can determine whether or not that person saw one of your Facebook ads. So, if you're looking for a 1:1 attribution from a Facebook ad, you may not see that. However, you can determine that it influenced an online gift.

5. **Online Display Ads:** Online display ads are notorious for not driving online gifts directly but are great for branding and

awareness. Retargeting ads are one of the better ways to get direct attribution because people seeing those ads have already visited your website. Similar to social media ads, online display ads should be viewed more as a support for fundraising campaigns, as opposed to a channel that will directly capture gifts. As a rule, to maximize success, these ads should never run by themselves without other campaign elements like email, social media, and website content.

6. **Content Marketing:** There's been a lot of chatter about content marketing in the last few years, and nonprofits are full of great stories that can make for extraordinary content. The challenge is taking those stories of impact that the nonprofit is making and turning them into images, posts, emails, blogs, and videos – and doing it consistently. Once you start, you have to keep feeding the monster, and that requires resources.

7. **Conversion Rate Optimization:** A newer but often overlooked tactic for digital fundraising is website CRO. This tactic focuses on the primary goals of converting website visitors into donors or email subscribers. This can be executed through exit-intent pop-ups, as well as dynamic content that can modify images and text based on specific website visitors instead of a one-size-fits-all website. For more information on this, check out Omniconvert, Optimizely, or Google Optimize.

8. **Bonus – Mobile/SMS:** Another channel to consider is mobile/SMS due to the sheer scale of donors with devices. The challenge, though, is that outside of text-to-give during disasters and events, this channel has yet to be proven as a highly effective standard for fundraising.

Why is this important? If you look at the fundraising landscape for nonprofits, many still obtain most of their donations through direct mail. This is how it was five years ago, and this is how it will be five years from now. I expect the scales to tip a little more toward digital fundraising over the next several years. Prioritizing your channels is important – as you obtain more donations online, you are maximizing opportunities while minimizing resources to acquire online gifts.

12

Campaign Overview & Final Notes

Digital Campaigns Overview

Everything that we've talked about in the book so far has all led to the execution of digital fundraising campaigns. This is the *Digital Fundraising Blueprint,* and you've learned about the digital ecosystem, how to plan your campaigns, and now it's time to review an example of how to execute a digital campaign. Campaigns typically follow one of three fundraising strategies: a) acquire new donors; b) retain existing donors; or c) grow the value of existing donors.

Digital campaigns are more frequently an extension of direct mail campaigns. This is because direct mail still holds the lion's share of revenue generated when it comes to fundraising. However, digital revenue is on the rise and growing at a faster rate than direct mail. Some nonprofits are now running separate digital campaigns that don't integrate with direct mail. One clear advantage of this is that you can learn quickly from a digital audience, especially with digital advertising, without investing in the cost of print production. You might even consider testing a campaign in digital and, based on the level of success, implement it next time with direct mail as well.

A fully integrated digital campaign has layers and complexities when it comes to channels, timing, monitoring, and reporting. In other words, there are a lot of eyes that need to be on each moving piece, in case adjustments are needed on the fly. To illustrate these layers, let's look at a hypothetical campaign, the channels you can use with the campaign, and how it all integrates. Imagine we're running a campaign for the month of October (though it could be any month) of any given year. Here's how the campaign might integrate:

Campaign duration: October 1-31

- **Website:**
  - *October 1* – Website banner (hero image) with campaign creative goes live to promote campaign.
- **Donation Page:**
  - *October 1* – Donation page has been previously tested and launches this day. It contains campaign image and copy above donation form fields.
- **Email:**
  - *October 1* – First email goes out announcing campaign, including campaign image and copy.
    - *October 8* – Resend original email with a different subject line to recipients of original email that did not open that email (non-openers).
    - *October 15* – Send second email in the campaign series. This email contains campaign theme, but may also include a video, infographic, or campaign update.
    - *October 31* – Send third and final email announcing campaign end. If possible, use a live countdown timer to create urgency.
    - *Note: All subsequent emails after the first one should only go to email subscribers that have not donated.*
- **Social Media Ads:**
  - *October 1* – Launch ads on Facebook and any other social media channels that feature campaign images and copy.

- *Note: Refresh creative weekly for ads and run through October 31.*
- *Tip: Segment ads with versioned copy specifically for your donors, lapsed donors, and prospective donor audiences.*

- **Social Media Content:**
  - *October 1* – Make a post on your social media channels, preferably an image or video, about the kick-off of the campaign.
  - Post 2-3 times a week for the rest of the month about services or benefits of the campaign.

- **SEM:**
  - *October 1* – Launch ads on Google and Bing to promote campaign and run through October 31.
  - *Tip: Create at least 6 different ads to determine which one converts the highest.*

- **Online Display Ads:**
  - *October 1* – Launch online display ads and run through October 31.
  - *Note: Create 2 different sets of ads and swap creative on October 15 to alleviate ad fatigue.*
  - *Tip: Use display ads to retarget traffic that visited your website or abandoned your donation page.*

- **SMS:**
  - *October 1* – Send SMS to subscribers to announce campaign and include a link to donate.
  - *October 15* – Send SMS to provide update of campaign, along with an affirmation message (no donation ask).
  - *October 31* – Send SMS announcing last day to give to campaign.

- **Other:**
    - Depending on your campaign, you may try to obtain media coverage on local news channels and newspapers.
    - Is there a peer-to-peer or digital catalog opportunity with this campaign?
    - Would there be an opportunity for you to use Snapchat or Facebook Live to kick off or provide updates on your campaign?
- **Direct Mail:**
    - In-home date should hit after campaign kicks off, preferably the first or second week of October.

As you can imagine, to pull off a campaign that uses this many marketing channels takes considerable planning, time, and resources. Don't be discouraged if you're not able to do everything listed here. Many campaigns don't require this many touchpoints, but certainly they would benefit your fourth quarter campaigns. You'll have to make that judgment call as far as what's possible based on your budget, resources, and skill sets.

I imagine your nonprofit is already involved to some degree in digital fundraising. Whether your organization is new to it or has been doing it for years, I'd like to leave you with some thought starters for different types of campaigns. Depending on where you are on the spectrum of maturity when it comes to digital fundraising, some of these ideas may seem like no-brainers. At any level, you can still take away some ideas and add them to your mix in the upcoming year.

- **Giving Tuesday:** More and more nonprofits are joining Giving Tuesday, which is the Tuesday following Thanksgiving. Over the last few years, the trend has been that small and medium-sized nonprofits have benefited the most. It's not to say that larger, national nonprofits aren't generating revenue

167

on this day; however, the year-over-year growth is larger with smaller and mid-sized nonprofits. Consider sending an email in the morning and evening on Giving Tuesday in order to maximize visibility in your subscribers' Inbox. Challenge your organization to continue to build out Giving Tuesday with new tactics like a "save the date" direct mail postcard, Facebook Live on Giving Tuesday, or Thank You email or social media post following Giving Tuesday.

- **Holiday Campaigns:** Whether you're a religious organization or not, the holiday season of November and December is a great time to capitalize on the generosity and overall increased giving during that time of year. Utilize language like, *"this holiday season..."* to provide relevance to your messaging.

- **Year-End Campaign:** Some nonprofits start Year-End digital campaigns the day after Christmas, while others wait until December 28 or 29. Either way, this is crunch time to raise money before the year ends and donors can benefit from the tax incentives that come along with donating to nonprofits. I've seen Year-End Campaigns generate more money than Thanksgiving or Christmas campaigns, which is pretty amazing considering the length of the campaign is only a few days. Whenever you decide to start your Year-End campaign, you'll help drive success by sending an email on December 29 or 30 and two emails on December 31 (one in the morning, one in the early evening). You'll want to communicate urgency in these emails and even include a live countdown timer, if possible.

- **Sustainer Campaign:** Sustaining donors are quite valuable to nonprofits. They help provide money to the organization on a consistent basis, whether that's monthly or quarterly. As such, it's worth planning at least one or more Sustainer campaigns per year. You can execute this via email, social media ads, and website banners. If possible, give donors an option on the donation page to make a gift monthly or quarterly. I believe a big opportunity exists for organizations to grow their number of sustainers. Many donors are already participating in sustainer programs without realizing it. What do you think Netflix is? A subscription service (sustainer program) that hits the bill each month for about $10. How can you create and position a sustainer offer to do the same and generate incremental revenue for your organization?

- **Volunteer Campaign:** Many organizations struggle with obtaining volunteers. Sure, they may have a page on the website where people can sign up to volunteer, but it's not actively marketed. You can put together a campaign that is calling for volunteers, which can be executed through email, website banners, social media ads, and social media posts. In the email, you can also provide the option of making a donation in the event the person is not able to volunteer time. I've seen this tactic be effective in generating both money and volunteers. Give it a try!

- **Affirmation Campaign:** It's important to balance out your fundraising communication with affirmational communication. If the only time your audience hears from you is when you're asking for money, then that's a problem. This is where you can send e-newsletters or emails that contain infographics, images, or stories of impact. If you have a great video, you can create a campaign around it that shows donors what they've made possible. Because these campaigns are affirmational in nature, use discretion as to whether or not you want to put paid advertising behind it. On the one hand, it's an affirmational video and not tied to fundraising. On the other hand, it helps to get your message out and may help generate additional gifts. This could be a testing opportunity for your organization to see what works best.

- **Disaster Response Campaign:** I've found that disaster response is an overlooked campaign opportunity for many organizations. If your nonprofit in any way helps out with feeding, shelter, donation of goods, or even animal care, then you may consider having a disaster campaign prepped and ready to execute when a disaster occurs. The demand for all of these services goes up in areas impacted by disaster. You might even consider using tactics like Facebook Live during times of disaster to show how your organization is involved. Timing is extremely important during disaster scenarios, so don't wait until it happens to start planning. You should have templates already built for emails, social media posts, and digital ads, ready to execute at short notice.

- **Digital Campaigns for In-Person Events:** If you have an in-person event like a 5K run, fundraising luncheon, or gala, then consider using digital channels to help promote or fundraise for these events. This can be done through emails, website banners, Facebook events, social media posts, social media ads, and peer-to-peer fundraising platforms. At the event, you can utilize mobile giving as well. Because you will likely have a captive audience, walk your attendees through the process of how to make a gift via mobile device. You will earn more money this way if you are intentional about it and literally provide step-by-step directions.

- **Giving Day:** More and more organizations are starting to have their own giving day, which raises money specifically during a 24-hour period. This is kind of like Giving Tuesday, but done during a different day of the year, specific to an individual organization. A giving day can commemorate the founding day of the nonprofit, or even coincide with a month where attention is put on the cause your nonprofit supports (e.g., National Domestic Violence Awareness Month). You can run it in a similar way to Giving Tuesday by serving up Facebook Ads, emails, direct mail "save-the-date" postcards, Facebook

Live, and other tactics. You may even be able to obtain some local media attention to help this day be even more successful. If you decide to have your own giving day, make sure you send out a "thank you" email and post on social media following the event to let your donors and advocates know how much money they helped raise.

Putting It into Practice

The *Digital Fundraising Blueprint* is just that, a blueprint. It's a starting point for you to build fundraising success. The knowledge, tips, and tactics in this book are designed to save you time in building frameworks from scratch. They are built on battle-tested executions that have helped generate over $100 million for nonprofits. It's up to you to build out the success of your own digital fundraising program and reference this blueprint along the way.

My goal for this book is to help your nonprofit do more good in the world. My hope is that you are now armed with enough information to understand the concepts of digital fundraising. This will help you ask the right questions and take your digital programs to the next level. The material in this book should help you identify quick wins you can put into place immediately and discover ideas to develop over a longer period of time. One thing is certain; digital is here to stay. Direct mail will still be the king of individual giving for the near future, but now is the time to position your nonprofit for relevancy and success 5, 10, and 20 years down the road. Without implementing a digital fundraising plan, you're leaving money on the table.

The months it takes in preparation of hitting the "go" button on your digital campaigns can be long and tedious. It can be filled with unexpected roadblocks with internal politics, technology, staffing, and more. However, when executed flawlessly, it can also be as beautiful as watching a symphony, each component playing its part according to plan. It's really exciting to check those revenue reports after your campaign begins. You see the fruits of your labor pay off. You see the lives that you're about to transform because of the money you helped raise. There's not many emotions that can match the joy of *knowing* you've made a difference in the world. It's why you selflessly work for a nonprofit, when you could likely get paid more doing the same kind of work for a commercial company. You care. You matter. You're awesome. Thank you for everything you do to make the world a better place.

####

Thanks for taking the time to read this book! If you're looking for a deeper understanding on digital fundraising, you can take Jeremy's online course, Digital Fundraising Blueprint, available at www.DigitalFundraisingBlueprint.com.

Full participation in the Digital Fundraising Blueprint online course is applicable for 4.5 points in Category 1.B – Education of the CFRE International application for initial certification and/or recertification.

Participation in the Digital Fundraising Blueprint may assist you in learning or reviewing concepts covered on the Certified Fund Raising Executive (CFRE) examination as detailed on the Test Content Outline provided by CFRE International. CFRE International does not sponsor or endorse any educational programs and the Digital Fundraising Blueprint was not developed in conjunction with CFRE International.

DIGITAL FUNDRAISING BLUEPRINT

Connect with Jeremy online at the following sites:
Website: www.JeremyHaselwood.com
Facebook: www.Facebook.com/JeremyHaselwood
Twitter: www.Twitter.com/JeremyHaselwood
Medium: www.Medium.com/@JeremyHaselwood

About Jeremy

Jeremy Haselwood is a marketing and business expert with over 20 years of experience working with commercial brands like Coca-Cola and nonprofits like The Salvation Army. He holds a Bachelor's degree in Marketing from Georgia State University and a MBA from Kennesaw State University. He has contributed articles to Forbes.com about personal development and digital fundraising.

Jeremy led digital strategies for nonprofit organizations in the realm of human services, animal care, healthcare, food banks, rescue missions, disaster response and more. His experience with nonprofits steered him to create the *Digital Fundraising Blueprint* online course and this book.

In addition, Jeremy combined his years of research and life experience, creating a personal development program called *"E.D.G.E. Academy."* In this training, he teaches how to maximize your talent and purpose to achieve a more fulfilled life. He's based in Atlanta, Georgia, where he lives with his wonderful wife and three kids.

Learn more at www.JeremyHaselwood.com